# FRENCH
# SOCIETY
# AND
# CULTURE

LIONEL GOSSMAN

The Johns Hopkins University

# FRENCH SOCIETY AND CULTURE

## Background for 18th Century Literature

Prentice-Hall, Inc., Englewood Cliffs, New Jersey

Library of Congress Catalog Card Number: 75-172404

Printed in the United States of America

ISBN: 0-13-331298-4

10 9 8 7 6 5 4 3 2 1

Prentice-Hall International, Inc., *London*
Prentice-Hall of Australia, Pty. Ltd., *Sydney*
Prentice-Hall of Canada, Ltd., *Toronto*
Prentice-Hall of India Private Limited, *New Delhi*
Prentice-Hall of Japan, Inc., *Tokyo*

# CONTENTS

# PREFACE

The history of philosophy and the history of literature are relatively recent disciplines. Both arose around the turn of the seventeenth and eighteenth centuries. From the beginning there was uncertainty as to whether they should be treated as autonomous spheres or studied in relation to the organization of society. Many of the great thinkers of the Enlightenment inclined to the second position. But the attempt to relate the cultural forms by which a society seeks to attain consciousness of itself and of the world to the forms of organization by which it secures its subsistence and continued existence has never met with unqualified success. No method of study has been evolved which can claim the rigor even of some humanistic disciplines, such as linguistics or philosophy.

The difficulty appears to be twofold. To claim that we have understood the relation between social organization and culture supposes that we have grasped the totality of the life of a society and that the principles by which its various aspects are related are known to us. This is a large assumption, particularly in the case of complex modern societies. In addition, both the claim that such understanding can be attained and the specific form in which it is realized are themselves part of culture.

The difficulty of establishing the relation between culture and society need not discourage us from trying, however. Even if the results are not definitive and the methods lack rigor, the effort itself contributes to our awareness of the complexity of the relations among the different levels of social life. The interaction of politics, economics, and culture is a topic of growing concern among students of literature and history today. This book is primarily addressed to them.

All organization and selection of material involves a point of view. I have tried both to make my own point of view explicit and to furnish the reader with sufficient material to adopt a different one. My aim has been to provide the student of literature with the means of constructing for himself an image of the society in and for which the literature of eighteenth-century France was produced. At the same time, I have sought to indicate some ways in which literature and ideas might be relevant to the concerns of the student of history.

The first two chapters deal largely with social history. I have tried to keep them abreast of current research and scholarship. In the third chapter I have outlined the history of ideas in the eighteenth century. I have also proposed an interpretation of the Enlightenment which some might dispute. The first part of the final chapter takes up the general problem of the relation of culture—especially literature—to society. The second part focusses on eighteenth-century French literature and illustrates from specific works and writers the ways in which this literature was both part of and opposed to a civilization characterized by hierarchies of power and authority.

LIONEL GOSSMAN
*Baltimore, Maryland*

# FRENCH
# SOCIETY
# AND
# CULTURE

Chapter **1**

# FRANCE:
# THE LAND
# AND
# THE PEOPLE

By the beginning of the eighteenth century France already had, more or less, its modern frontiers and it was, as it still is, one of the largest countries in Europe. In addition, it was then the most populous. Only the loosely strung Austrian empire could rival France with its 20 million inhabitants. England and Spain with 5 million each were no match, and even Russia with 14 million could not compete with it. Of these 20 million, by far the largest number lived on and by the land.[1] There were only two towns of any size, by modern standards, in all France: Paris with about half a million inhabitants—the only comparable city in Europe at the time was London with about 700,000—and Lyons with about 130,000. Five towns could count more than 50,000 inhabitants—Marseille, Bordeaux, Rouen, Lille, and Nantes—and in a nonurban society these were large cities indeed. The other French towns were small. Even an important administrative and cultural center like Dijon could boast only 20,000 inhabitants in 1785.[2] There was a real difference between townspeople and countrypeople. In some parts of Europe the difference might be one of language and religion, as in eastern Europe, where the town dwellers were Jews, Germans, or Italians in a Slavic or Magyar sea. In France, although there were no religious or ethnic differences, townsfolk enjoyed various fiscal privileges that marked them off from countryfolk. They were exempt, for instance, from the *taille* and the *corvée* and in large measure from military service.[3] Moreover, they looked different. They wore different clothes and they were also generally taller. They tended, in addition,

1

to be quicker witted and more literate. The distinction that the bourgeois philosophers liked to draw between *philosophes* and *peuple*[4] corresponds in some measure to that between the enterprising and open-minded townsman and the peasant locked in centuries-old routines. Within the towns themselves, of course, there were divisions between the bourgeois and the workingman, between the more or less enterprising tradesman or merchant and the routine-bound artisan.

The most dynamic towns were in fact those that were open to the sea, for it was overseas trade that was expanding rapidly in the seventeenth and eighteenth centuries, not domestic trade; and the merchants or *armateurs* of Bordeaux, Nantes, Rouen, Le Havre were among the most energetic elements of the French population. The inland towns also benefited somewhat from improved road and, to a lesser degree, water communications, and their inhabitants lived distinctly urban lives. But the inland town still lived off its surrounding countryside to a very large extent. Its bourgeois were dealers in corn or cattle, processors of farm produce, lawyers and notaries handling the affairs of noble estates or the interminable litigations that are characteristic of landowning societies, and occasionally merchant entrepreneurs who put the rural population to work by furnishing the raw materials or the rudimentary equipment for spinning and weaving. Its shopkeepers and artisans supplied the surrounding peasantry as well as the townsfolk who were living off the peasantry. Not unexpectedly, the inland city clung jealously to its domination of the local market and did not always unreservedly favor "progressive" movements aimed at breaking down local barriers and monopolies. Though it represented a different way of life from that of the peasant or farmer, it remained bound to the countryside that sustained it.

And in the countryside change was very slow indeed. Agriculture, by far the dominant sector of the French economy and the occupation of the vast majority of the population—as it was in all the other countries of Europe—was pursued much as it had been for centuries. In England and Holland some new techniques had been introduced, but they were slow to catch on; likewise new crops had been brought to Europe from overseas—corn, rice, potatoes—but farmers proved conservative and clung to the crops traditionally cultivated in their region.[5] There were, in short, few opportunities for improvement in agriculture and in France these few were not much exploited, partly because of the system of land tenure.[6] Colbert had hardly included agriculture in his programs. He placed his hopes for the improvement of rural conditions on industry.

Since most people lived either on the land or in close contact with it, it is not surprising that for the majority of Frenchmen at the beginning of the eighteenth century life remained substantially what it had been in the days of their grandfathers and great-grandfathers. The family structure was stable, with the father firmly at its head and supported in that position by the law and the state. (Diderot's father, for instance, though he was only a well-to-do artisan, found no difficulty in having his son shut up in a monastery when he threatened to marry a girl Didier Diderot disapproved of. Reader's of Prevost's *Manon Lescaut* will recall the ease with which des Grieux's father got the authorities to act on his behalf. There are similar episodes in other eighteenth-century novels.) Collective family responsibility persisted, in fact, until well into the eighteenth century, so that the father of Damiens, the youth who attempted to assassinate Louis XV, had to go into exile on account of his son's crime. Children often continued to live with their parents after marriage, and for as long as they did so, they remained subject to paternal authority.[7]

The population itself was relatively stable. Crises, such as bad harvests, famines, epidemics, wars, might cause a sudden unusually high mortality or a drop in fertility, but with better times the losses would be made good again. The French population had fluctuated round the 20 million mark since the fourteenth century.[8] No wonder Colbert could not conceive of an expanding market, but only of acquiring a larger share of an existing market for French commerce. "Les peuples sont toujours égaux en nombre dans tous les états," he affirmed, "et  .  .  .  pareillement la consommation est toujours égale."[9] In this relatively static world a moderate fertility rate was accompanied by a high mortality rate and low life expectancy.[10] There were few large families. Only about one in twenty-five had more than six children, according to contemporary statistics. In one area, it was calculated that between 1760 and 1790 43 percent of the children died before reaching the age of ten, and of these 20 percent died in infancy. At Lyons, where working women gave their children out to wet nurses in the country so that they could stay on the job, infant mortality is said to have been 4,000 in 1778, the number of live births 6,000. Many babies were abandoned by parents unable to raise them, especially in the urban areas. In 1788 statistics for Paris show more than 5,800 abandoned infants for 20,000 baptisms. The low life expectancy of the time—about thirty to thirty-five at birth in the country, rather less in the towns, and markedly less among the urban lower classes than among the well-to-do —is revealed in the age structure of the population. In 1775, of every 1,000 persons 426 were aged up to nineteen, 309 twenty to thirty-nine, 194 forty to fifty-nine, and only 71 sixty or over.[11] Moreover, the quality of the population was not high; a low standard of mental as well as physical health prevailed, particularly in the less-salubrious provinces.

The France into which Voltaire, Montesquieu, and Diderot were born was thus a slow-moving society, still largely subject to the rhythms of nature. Indeed a history of the climate of the seventeenth and eighteenth centuries would be an important part of any general history. Communications had been improved, but over a very narrow range. Few people left the closed confines of the place where they were born and for the vast majority movement was measured best by the speed of the carter walking beside his horse or mule. Letters were carried more regularly and more speedily than ever—and the eighteenth century was a great age of correspondence—but it was only a small proportion of the population that ever wrote or received one. Fewer people than one might think were absolutely illiterate, but education was rudimentary for most people and did not go far beyond learning their catechism.[12] In commerce and industry, only luxury trades or those trades that interested the army and navy developed rapidly, not the production and exchange of everyday articles for the mass of the people.[13] The idea of *exchange* was to dominate eighteenth-century literature and thought, and the word *commerce* was a favorite one with the philosophers, but both the commerce of goods and the commerce of ideas in the early eighteenth century concerned the thin upper crust of the population. The vast mass below, the *peuple,* as it was referred to by bourgeois and aristocrats alike, continued to live more or less as it had for generation upon generation.

In the course of the century, however, the great body of France began to move. A marked demographic upthrust and an equally notable economic upturn just before mid-century shook the power of routine. Writers and philosophers tried to provide new categories by means of which the new reality could be mastered conceptually; in turn, this new consciousness enhanced the possibility of rational control and modification of the environment. As often happens, an accelerating rate of social change was accompanied by an increased awareness of social organization and an ever more vocal demand for social reform. The traditional structure of society became the object of vehement criticism.

Traditionalist and slow-changing as it was, France at the beginning of the eighteenth century was nevertheless a different place from the France of the Middle Ages. No doubt it was still a "feudal" state,[14] but the "feudalism" of the seventeenth and eighteenth centuries was by no means identical with that of the High Middle Ages.

There are several interpretations of the significance of the royal absolutism that from the middle of the seventeenth century on overlaid the feudal structure of France. Traditionally the monarchy is thought of as an autonomous political force that allied itself with the bourgeoisie and was thus able to overcome the resistance of the feudal nobility. This theory was already popular in the eighteenth century itself. Some members of the nobility who were interested in regaining power by weakening the monarchy saw in the latter the ally of the bourgeoisie (Boulainviller, for example); the bourgeois in some measure concurred and hoped that the monarchy would continue to fulfill its "historical role" by implementing the policies and programs they desired (Voltaire). More recently it has been argued that the monarchy was the instrument of power of a self-interested and self-perpetuating bureaucracy.

The Russian historian Boris Porshnev has questioned both these views. According to him a political power cannot be "pure"; it must represent the interests of some social class. The absolute monarchy cannot therefore be considered an autonomous force in French politics, nor can it be considered the instrument of a social group such as a bureaucracy, which Porshnev would doubtless classify as a subgroup within a social class. Instead of relating the monarchy to the *tiers* or the bourgeoisie, however, Porshnev sees it as at all times the instrument by which an often uncomprehending nobility was maintained in being and saved from its own destructive factions and intrigues.[15] Concessions had to be made, Porshnev admits, to the bourgeoisie, which was to furnish the administrative cadres and a good deal of the finances of the new regime. The monarchy could satisfy its pensioned nobility and maintain the state only by encouraging trade and commerce and drawing revenues from them. The only alternative source of revenue was the peasantry, and to get money from that already hard-pressed source the crown would have had to enter into direct competition with the landowning nobility, which also milched the peasants as best it could.

The demand for money was so pressing, however, that the government had to resort to many short-term measures, which tended to undermine its own long-term plans. Porshnev describes the dilemma the monarchy found itself in at some length. Encouraging trade and commerce, on the one hand, it tended on the other to draw the active merchant class into the class of *officiers* by offering for sale various legal and administrative posts, carrying noble privileges and exemptions of one kind or another. It thus weakened and offended the established nobility by creating a rival class, the so-called *noblesse de robe,* and at the same time it undercut its own efforts to stimulate commerce and to build up a sound civil service. Only by giving up the easy and immediate revenues provided by the sale of offices, and by reducing taxes on income from trade and commerce could it have kept the bourgeoisie in its place and discouraged the transfer of capital out of commerce. But it could not afford to do either. It was thus not only vanity that led the French bourgeois to invest in *offices,* titles, lands and *rentes* (government bonds and other fairly safe loans). It was also the desire to put his money out of reach of the fisc.

The crown's efforts to make money out of the sale of titles and privileges made it more and more patent that their meaning and social function bore little resemblance to those that were attributed to them in the feudal ideology. Titles and offices were no more than a kind of investment, a form of movable property. Absolutism replaced or at least reinforced the early feudal system of government, on which the system of privileges rested, with a "modern," centralized administration, and at the same time it changed the social meaning of privilege. Moreover, the administration itself had to be continually renewed as its posts were transformed into sinecures and its personnel entered the ranks of the privileged. The latter were thus constantly swollen by an endless flood of new recruits.

The persistence of old forms in altered social and economic conditions is typical of the last two centuries of the Old Regime, and it was the cause of serious conflicts. We shall find it in the system of land tenure and in the tax system as well as in the class structure of society. As we explore these areas, however, we should bear in mind that any generalizations about them must be sketchy. Right into the eighteenth century, France remained a country of regions and provinces, each with its own social, economic, institutional, and even in some cases linguistic character (Brittany and Languedoc, for instance, were not yet fully francophone). The area around Paris, together with Normandy and Picardy was, on the whole, an area whose economy was open, whose commercial activity was active and whose relatively dense population included large numbers of rural artisans; the Mediterranean area was far more closed and economically independent. As one historian has remarked, "On est encore, au XVII$^e$ siècle, assez près du cloisonnement féodaliste ancien; de nombreux pays restent à l'écart des grands axes commerciaux."[16]

Let us glance first at the system of land tenure.

The Russian historian Loutchisky was the first to draw attention to the peculiar nature of the agrarian system in France as compared with that of England on the one hand or of eastern Europe on the other. In eastern Europe, the land remained almost entirely in the hands of great feudal lords who exploited it themselves by means of the corvées that the peasants, almost all of them serfs, owed to him. In England, serfdom, corvées, and most feudal rights had disappeared by the end of the Middle Ages; land rent remained, but between the sixteenth and eighteenth centuries the peasants who paid it were evicted by one means or another. Very large farms could then be constituted, which the landowners worked, rather efficiently, by means of hired labor. The English peasants were thus free, but landless, and the land was increasingly subject to capitalist methods of exploitation. In France the peasants were free as in England, but a large number, even among the *journaliers,* so called because they hired out their labor by the day, owned a plot of land of some size. It has been estimated that in 1789 an average of 30–40 percent of the land in France was peasant property, though the percentage varied from region to region.[17] Of course, many of these peasant holdings were very small.

Peasant tenure in the eighteenth century was hereditary. The peasant could not be deprived of the land he held, except for nonpayment of dues, and he was free, moreover, to sell it, bequeath it, or lease it out as he pleased. Although the landlord held what the lawyers called *propriété éminente* over lands thus tenanted, the peasant was sensibly considered to have *propriété utile* over it. The form in which the dues owed to the landlord were paid varied. In northern France payment was mostly in the form of money, and as the value of money declined steadily, the landlord was eager to recoup whatever lands he could for nonpayment of dues so as to let them out again more profitably.[18] The landlord's own estate was indeed often farmed by being leased to local peasants for stipulated periods at varying rates. As few peasants had enough land of their own, the demand for leases was greater than the supply and they generally fetched a good price. In fact, landlords were encouraged, by the good returns on these leases and by their own continually increasing expenses, to clear more and more of their woodlands and grab as much as they could of the common lands in their area, which they enclosed and then farmed out to the peasants. This tendency became very marked toward the end of the *ancien régime*.

The old feudal relations of lord and tenant thus preserved little of their earlier character. They had become impersonal and commercial, the more so as the landlords themselves changed frequently, especially in the neighborhood of towns. The seigneurial dues and feudal customs that persisted were likewise exploited coldly and realistically, increasingly so toward the end of the century. Indeed many such dues,—*cens* in wine, grain, hay, oil, chickens, and so on, payment for the use of the lord's mills and ovens (even if they were not actually used), dues on legal contracts, taxes on markets and fairs—were themselves farmed out by the landlord, who was interested only in the cash to be got from them.[19]

If seigneurial rights had lost their personal character and had become mere sources of income for impersonal (often absent or changing) landlords, old feudal customs that turned out to be inefficient or costly but that helped the poor to stay alive—*glanage, droit de chaume, vaine pâture, jouissance des communaux*—were considered "abuses" by the landlords and wealthier peasants and frequent appeals were made to have them abolished.[20]

On the one hand, therefore, a system of land tenure that allowed the peasant virtual ownership of his land, on the other, the persistence of old feudal dues that were increasingly exploited with a harshness and impersonality characteristic of capitalist rather than feudal social relations; on the one hand, elements of a structure inherited from feudalism, on the other, an outlook among richer peasants as well as among the wealthy possessors of seigneurial lands more akin to that of the entrepreneur than to that of the feudal lord and his serfs.[21]

Characteristically the tax system of the ancien régime was extremely uneven. It functioned differently from province to province. It applied differently to different members of the same social order. The various principalities that had been gradually annexed to the French crown retained in varying degrees their historic rights. In some provinces the tax fell upon land, in others upon persons. In some places the salt monopoly was not applied, in others it was applied moderately, in still others it was rigorously enforced. Goods passing from one province to another were subject to duties of all kinds. Even liberally minded men withdrew before the increasingly loud demands that uniformity be brought to the complicated fiscal system of the ancien régime. "Against any efforts to do so," wrote Necker, the finance minister of Louis XVI, "some of the privileged provinces would hold up rights inscribed in the treaty by which they were united to France, others the document by which they once bought themselves out of taxation and the customs established over several centuries. We must recognize, however, that agreements entered into with the provinces are no less valid and binding than other promises made by sovereigns: everything is held together in great societies by the bonds of justice and law."[22]

The division of the population into privileged and nonprivileged classes in the ancien régime, the former being exempt from most taxes, was also an inheritance from the feudal past. As *gens de service* were considered nontaxable in the Middle Ages, payment of personal taxes or taxes on land became a sign of servile condition, and something of this persisted throughout the ancien régime. The royal administration never dared to raise the question of a general tax on all immovable estate and sought to make up its needs partly by the sale of offices and titles of nobility, but mostly by extending the system of indirect taxes and by raising taxes on consumer articles. The lower orders alone were subject to the taille, which in the south of France, where Roman law held sway, affected the land, and in the north, the land of custom law, affected the producer himself. Noble lands in the south and noblemen themselves in the north were exempted from the tax, which thus fell solely on the nonprivileged. But the very manner in which the taille was raised was arbitrary. The well-to-do bourgeois farming land around the towns could always buy exemption by acquiring a title of nobility. Moreover the collectors, appointed from the population of the rural communities themselves, were personally responsible for nonpayment: they therefore ensured themselves against loss by taxing themselves and their families very lightly and by trying to have the defenseless taxed highly, whereas the crafty or those with influential support got off lightly. As taxes were assessed according to external signs of wealth, there was room for even more abuse. (The case of the peasant in Rousseau's *Confessions,* pleading poverty until he was sure that the traveler was not an agent of the fisc in disguise, comes immediately to mind.) Still another irregularity was introduced by the local noblemen who contrived to have the assessment of their lease farmers reduced and the difference applied to their tenant farmers. The tax collectors could, of course, be brought to justice, but only very wealthy peasants could afford to become embroiled in the expenses of a lawsuit.

The taxes on consumer goods affected everybody, of course, but they fell most heavily on the poorer members of society. Wheat, the staple of the French peasant, was subject to many duties as it was transported from one province to another, in addition to the seigneurial dues of *péage* and *pontage.* Wine was similarly taxed. The economic reformer Le Trosne claimed that a shipment of wine from Roussillon or Languedoc in south-western France would be subject to thirty-five or forty different dues before reaching Paris.[23] The smugglers in Diderot's story *Les Deux Amis de Bourbonne* had a basis in social reality. The state monopolies—on tobacco, and especially on salt—were another source of income to the royal exchequer that was particularly vexatious to the peasant. Salt was a necessity not simply for seasoning food, but above all for preserving it—and not only human food, but also the fodder of sheep and plow animals. It thus directly affected the peasant's livelihood. As the salt tax was heavy, the peasant was naturally tempted to get it from illegal sources. In 1784 Necker reckoned that a third of the prison population was made up of smugglers: every year, he wrote, 2,300 men, 1,800 women, and 6,000 children are arrested for illegal transportation of salt.[24] The state monopoly met this difficulty by stipulating an amount of salt that the peasant was expected to need and to purchase from official sources. In addition to the taxes mentioned, there were, of course, many others, which were levied at various stages on the road from producer to consumer.

The state itself did not always get the most out of these various taxes. Chronically short of funds, it had to farm out the indirect taxes to syndicates of financiers. The amount advanced by the latter was always far less than the amount recovered by the agents of the tax farm and huge profits were made by individuals. The taxes of the state were thus themselves a commercial property on which capitalists could and did speculate.

In the course of the eighteenth century new and theoretically more equitable taxes were introduced, but in the end they were successfully resisted by the forces of privileges—social classes, corporate bodies such as the church, whole provinces. In the long run the government had to yield to these forces, since it could not survive without the support of the very society it was there to sustain. In the end, therefore, the new taxes simply added to the burden of the existing taxpayers.

## SOCIAL CLASSES

The society of the ancien régime is traditionally divided into three so-called orders or estates—clergy, nobility, and third estate. But these categories, which date from the Middle Ages, do not adequately describe the social reality of the last centuries of the ancient régime.[25] Contemporaries were aware that there was another, more significant division of society than the traditional one. The Dutch historian Pontanus, for instance, writing in 1606, divided France into three classes—nobility, bourgeoisie, and peuple.[26] The tiers alone included a number of classes with profoundly different interests. In the towns, as we shall see shortly, the upper bourgeoisie (financiers, bankers, members of the bar, holders of administrative offices), the middle bourgeoisie (merchants and tradespeople), the petty bourgeoisie (shopkeepers, artisans), and the lower classes (workers and employees), not to mention the large army of domestic servants and the vast population of vagrants and beggars, were in most significant respects more divided than united by their interests; likewise in the country there was conflict between the well-to-do peasants (laboureurs) and the poor journaliers who had only their labor to sell; and cutting across these differences there were those that separated townsfolk from countryfolk.

The nobility was hardly a single class with unified interests either. The poor hobereau of Brittany or southern France, working the land himself and struggling desperately to eke out a miserable living, had nothing in common with the wealthy and well-pensioned court aristocrat or even with his better off counterparts in other areas. (Readers of Marivaux will recall a series of dramatic conflicts between poor rural nobility and rich urban aristocracy in La Vie de Marianne, notably in the story of Tervire.) As for the clergy, far from being a single unified order, it was rent by the same social conflicts that affected the rest of society. As part of the crown's policy of financially supporting the nobility, top ecclesiastical posts—as well as top posts in the army—were increasingly reserved for those who could prove their noble blood.[27] The dîme, a substantial tax payable to the church, went mostly to the bishops and the latter lived like princes, often, indeed, in Paris or at court, rather than in their dioceses. Their class feelings ran deep. Christophe de Beaumont, the bishop of Paris who was the recipient of a famous open letter from Rousseau, admitted no parish priests to his table, and this behavior was not uncommon. The parish priest, on the other hand, often lived like a peasant, and felt closer to his flock than to the princes of the church. The dissensions that beset the church in the eighteenth century were not unrelated to these social divisions within it.[28]

The pioneer social historian Henri Sée based his analysis of the society of the ancien régime on a distinction between holders of movable and holders of immovable property. We shall content ourselves here with describing as briefly as possible the richly varied social composition of two of the so-called estates—the nobility and the tiers—in order to bring out the gap between traditional categories and the social reality that they were less and less able to account for effectively.

## THE NOBILITY

It is hard to say how numerous the nobility was in the last century of the ancien régime. Vauban's figure was as high as 200,000; the genealogist Cherin estimated about 80,000; Expilly calculated 78,000; Siéyès 110,000. One of the reasons for the insufficiency of these estimates is the difficulty of defining the nobility. "Au lieu d'une noblesse il y en avait sept ou huit," Talleyrand was to remark: "une d'épée et une de robe, une de cour et une de province, une ancienne et une nouvelle, une grande et une petite."[29] Some contemporaries, particularly die-hards like Saint Simon, refused to recognize the *robins* as noble and continued to refer to them as bourgeois; yet it has been shown that by the eighteenth century the two nobilities of robe and sword were closer than ever in aims, values, and attitudes.[30] And what of the countless *anoblis,* administrators and financiers elevated to the nobility in the seventeenth or eighteenth century by marriage, purchase of titles or offices, or purchase of seigneurial lands?[31] Necker estimated that half the nobility in 1789 had acquired this status in the two preceding centuries and his estimate seems borne out by recent research.[32] Of 80,000 noble families, the marquis de Bouillé claimed, barely 1,000 could boast of origins going back to the first centuries of the French monarchy, and of these only about 200 or 300 were not indigent. In Brittany and southern France especially, the proportion of indigent noblemen was high,[33] but they were numerous everywhere.[34] Many of them, despised by the wealthier laboureurs but fiercely jealous of their prerogatives, lived like poor peasants and plowed their own land. Others, fearful of derogating, led a futile existence on the edge of poverty, unable to bring up their sons for any kind of public service or to provide for their daughters. Some even took to crime to support themselves. A recent study of criminal records has revealed that ruined hobereaux in the southwest kept up a state of endemic brigandage.[35] Rétif de La Bretonne describes in his own native province of Burgundy "des gentilshommes chasseurs, en guêtres, en souliers ferrés, portant sous le bras une vieille épée rouillée, mourant de faim et refusant de travailler."[36] In contrast, the court nobility and many of the anoblis lived lavishly. Likewise, the robins lived very well, if less ostentatiously.

The nobility was not in fact anything like a closed caste. From the Middle Ages on it had been possible for wealthy men to enter its ranks. In France this infiltration had been gradual and the feudal way of life seems to have absorbed the new members completely. Toward the end of the sixteenth century, however, the composition of the French nobility began to alter more rapidly. Money was beginning to class men more than the old distinctions of orders.[37] Hungry for wealth, the crown created many new offices in the administration of justice and of finance, and to make these attractive to buyers varying degrees of noble privilege and exemption from taxes were attached to them. It was no longer only the old nobility or the *grands officiers* who enjoyed the exemptions and privileges associated with nobility; a whole host of offices conferred a kind of seminobility. The holders of such offices were exempt from *franc-fief* (payable on purchase of noble lands by nonnobles) and from the obligation to lodge the king's soldiers. They paid neither taille nor *aides* (consumer taxes), could buy salt from the state at cost price, and were exempt from dîmes, *octrois,* and péages (taxes on transportation of goods). And later, when the *vingtième,* a new tax, payable by all, was introduced, the magistrates and officers got off lightly along with the rest of the nobility.[38] With the edict of La Paulette in 1584 many of these offices became fully inheritable. A new permanent aristocracy was thus created—the so-called *noblesse de robe*—detested by the old nobility which saw its privileged social position being usurped and by *roturiers* who were convinced that they had to pay more heavily to the exchequer to make up for the exemptions granted its erstwhile members. Many purchasers of offices ultimately acquired fiefs and their children and grandchildren lived like noblemen on their country estates. Students of literature will think of the example of the dramatist Regnard on his estate at Dourdan.[39] "L'office," Roland Mousnier put it, "est un moyen de parvenir, un passage."[40] By the eighteenth century there seem to have been about 4,000 purchasable offices carrying noble privileges. This figure includes 900 royal secretaryships, the emoluments from which were very small, so that the sole reason for purchasing such a post must have been to gain social status and tax exemptions.

A further measure that opened the ranks of the nobility to new blood was taken in 1614 when the purchase of fiefs by commoners—a practice that had, in fact, been going on for some time—was made legal. In France this measure was particularly important. The first ambition of the robe and the wealthy bourgeoisie was to purchase a fief and acquire the title of seigneur. There are countless cases of such ennoblements in the seventeenth and eighteenth centuries. One example will suffice. Pâris Montmartel, one of the four Pâris brothers who were among the outstanding financiers and statesmen of the eighteenth century, was the son of a poor innkeeper at Moirans. But he could later sign himself comte de Sampigny, baron de

Dagonville, seigneur de Brunoy, seigneur de Villers, seigneur de Foncy, seigneur de Fontaine, seigneur de Châteauneuf, and so on.

Louis XIV's expensive wars were an important factor in altering the composition and outlook of the nobility. The outright sale of titles of nobility became a means of refurbishing the treasury. Not that they were sold crudely on the open market. The king invited certain persons, distinguished for their services to the state—which often meant for providing loans—to purchase *lettres de noblesse*. Some 500 new nobles were created in this way in 1696, 200 in 1702, and another 100 in 1711.[41]

Marriage was one of the favorite methods by which wealthy commoners infiltrated the aristocracy. In the seventeenth century France entered a period of relative economic stagnation from which she began, very slowly, to recover only in the second quarter of the eighteenth century.[42] During this period the only people who did consistently well were the financiers, speculators and suppliers of food and equipment to the armed services. The price of wheat and wine, by which the economic health of the country can be determined, remained depressed with only minor fluctuations brought on by unusually bad harvests. Nor did these brief periods of higher prices help any but the wealthiest farmers. The majority could not time their sales to coincide with the better conditions, while the poorest had sometimes mortgaged their crop in advance in order to obtain seed. Inevitably land rent during this time remained fairly low, so that the nobleman was also hit. Even the court nobility occasionally felt the pinch. The pensions and lucrative secular and ecclesiastical positions on which they had been able to count and for which they vied with one another began to be dispensed less generously.[43] But the demands of court life did not abate, and many noble families got into serious debt. "Et croyez-vous qu'un homme de cour puisse être riche au temps où nous sommes?" asks one of the characters in Dancourt's *Le Chevalier à la mode* (1687). "Les courtisans malaisés ne s'enrichissent point; et ceux qui sont le plus à leur aise ne sont pas difficiles à ruiner" (III, ix). Few could turn down an alliance of their sons with the daughters of wealthy financiers. On learning of one such marriage the duchesse de Chaulnes is said to have remarked to her son: "Mon fils, ce mariage est bon; il faut bien que vous preniez du fumier pour engraisser vos terres."[44] The memoirs of the period are full of reports of such marriages. Some concerned people whose names are almost synonymous with the grace and charm of aristocratic life in eighteenth-century France. Anne Pléneuf married the marquis de Prie, became the mistress of the regent, the duc de Bourbon, and reigned supremely in that capacity over the society of the Regency. A daughter of the financier Antoine Crozat married into the ancient house of Bouillon and became comtesse d'Evreux. Crozat's second son, known as the baron de Thiers, married Mme de Laval-Montmorency and the daughters of their union married the marquis de Béthune and the maréchal de Broglie. The daughters of another financier, Samuel Bernard, who was himself feted by Louis XIV, married into the proud families of Môlé and Boulainviller. The duchesse du Maine, who ran one of the great salons of the Regency, was the daughter of the millionaire Abraham Peyrenc, a one-time barber. Madame de Pompadour herself was born Mlle Poisson. These commoners, despite the nasty things that envious people said about them, were often educated and cultured and they were great patrons of literature and the arts. The new aristocracy that resulted from their union with the old nobility was thus enriched in more ways than one. Above all, however, the alliance of the nobility with the world of business and finance gave it a new lease on life by restoring its fortunes. "La finance est alliée aujourd'-hui à la noblesse et voilà ce qui fait la base de sa force réelle," wrote a contemporary observer at the end of the eighteenth century.[45]

The *grande noblesse de robe*—about 1,100 top magistrates—appears to have been on the whole better off than the old nobility.[46] The Premier Président d'Aligre was said to have 5 million livres in the bank in London and an income of 700,000 livres (a livre is approximately equivalent to a U.S. dollar today). In the provinces the upper magistrates were also very rich and, above all, landed.[47] The families of great magistrates like the Bouhiers and the de Brosses in Burgundy held vast tracts of rich land and since the seventeenth century they had sought to maintain favorable conditions for themselves in the province. Thus they resisted the attempts of Colbert and the intendant Brulart to introduce cottage industry, since they feared a rise in the cost of labor.[48] In Languedoc the magistrates made up the wealthiest class of the population. The best vineyards in the Bordeaux area, for instance, were in robe hands—Laffite, Latour, Saint-Estèphe, Margaux, Haut-Brion. The greatest robe families carried noble titles and from their ranks came a host of ministers and secretaries of state, especially in the later seventeenth and eighteenth centuries. The comte de Saint-Florentin and the comte de Pontchartrain, both ministers of Louis XIV, and the comte de Maurepas, the astute minister of Louis XVI, were all from the robe family of Phelypeaux; the d'Argensons—although originally landed gentry—were likewise from a robe family, as were two other great eighteenth-century ministers, Machault d'Arnouville and Maupeou.

The magistrates were also hit by the economic crisis, of course. Moreover, the value of their offices declined dramatically in the course of the eighteenth century, partly because their own exclusiveness restricted the market.[49] But they still did fairly well from the *épices* paid to them by litigants, and some of them, notably the premiers présidents, received considerable sums from the Treasury, doubtless in return for influencing their *parlements* to act in accordance with the king's wish. In 1765 d'Aligre, premier président of the Parlement de Paris, was getting a pension of

10,000 *livres,* and in 1775 it was 20,000. But even the robe, which was, if anything, more envious and resentful of the financiers than the nobility, did not disdain alliance with them. Barbier relates that at the marriage of the son of Môlé, président à mortier of the Parlement de Paris, to the daughter of Samuel Bernard, the bride's dowry amounted to over a million livres.[50]

The transformation of the old nobility affected attitudes and ways of thinking even more than genealogies. The policies of the kings themselves, although designed in some ways, as we have seen, to save the nobility, had already had the effect of altering its character. As the nobles settled at court and abandoned to others the various social functions they had once exercised personally, their possessions and privileges came to be seen in a more and more cold and impersonal light as sources of revenue. The court nobles themselves were thus among the first to adopt a realistic "commercial" outlook. As early as the beginning of the seventeenth century, the marquis de Sully observed ruefully "que les idées sont changées et que l'or met le prix à tout. Et comment cela n'arriverait-il pas, puisqu'on voit la Noblesse elle-même penser sur cet article précisément comme le peuple."[51] The old personal and feudal relations persisted into the reigns of Henry IV and Louis XIII and there are still echoes of them even at the Court of Versailles,[52] but they counted for less and less. Meantime, as expenses rose and income suffered because of the crisis, noblemen began to take an increasingly active interest in money matters. "Ils sont dans la gêne," the historian Philippe Sagnac wrote, "et, en dépit de leurs habitudes et de leurs goûts, obligés maintenant de calculer."[53]

Since the time of Richelieu the participation of noblemen in overseas commerce and in industry was not considered a derogation and we find many of the court nobles taking advantage of the opportunities open to them. According to Savary, the author of a celebrated handbook of commerce, *Le parfaict Négociant* (1675), "la plupart des personnes de qualité, de robe et autres, donnent leur argent aux négociants en gros pour le faire valoir."[54] When the Compagnie de l'Orient was formed in 1642, one of the principal shareholders was the duc de La Meilleraye. In some areas noblemen were particularly active.[55] When the great Saint-Gobain glass and mirror works was founded in 1692 with a capital of 2 million livres, the majority of the shareholders were noblemen. Noble interests were also dominant in many of the other so-called *manufactures royales* (that is, industries enjoying government protection, special tax exemptions, and so on) as well as in mining and iron foundries, which were thought of as a kind of exploitation of the land and therefore appropriate to noblemen. The mines of Anzin, which by 1789 employed 4,000 workers together with twelve steam engines and 600 horses, were run by the marquis de Castres and the chevalier de Solages.[56] The duc de Noailles and the duc de La

Meilleraye also had mining interests. The iron industry could boast some of the greatest names in France in the eighteenth century: Lafayette, Caulaincourt, Choiseul-Gouffier, Bauffremont. Of 601 forge masters of determinable status, listed in the royal inquiries of 1771 and 1778, 60 percent were noblemen.[57] The number of noblemen who speculated on stocks was also considerable. Law's famous Mississippi Company alone caused many a fortune and many a title to be lost or acquired at the end of the second decade of the eighteenth century.[58] It is known that the duc d'Antin, the duc de La Force, and the maréchal d'Estrées made a fortune from speculation.

The state itself helped to alter the character of the nobility by the very measures it took to preserve it. In the end the form alone remained, whereas the content was profoundly different. The changed styles and techniques of modern warfare, the importance to the state of colonial adventures, and the vast bureaucratic system created or encouraged by the state made the old feudal arrangements appear more and more anachronistic, as some contemporaries, such as Boulainviller, could see. Louis XIV's wars demanded modern armies and modern equipment, not the seigneurial armies of old; his colonial ventures created new and powerful commercial interests; and the administration of the state required not feudal lords but a large body of well-trained, well-educated officials. When the king was in trouble he no longer called on his vassals; he called on Bernard the banker.

Certainly the state continued to favor the old nobility. The highest and most lucrative posts in the church were reserved, as we have already mentioned, for noblemen who could prove their ancient lineage. Similarly, in the army, commissions were seldom given to commoners: they were looked upon as the rightful prerogative of the nobility, its proper, indeed, its principal function. To assist poor noblemen who could not afford a regiment, new grades were created (lieutenant colonel and major) for which commissions could not be bought. Under Louis XVI commissions were made virtually unobtainable by any save those who could prove four generations of nobility. At court too the old nobility was favored. Nobody could be presented unless he could establish direct noble descent since 1400. The rule was relaxed from time to time, but rarely.[59] An elaborate etiquette, moreover, distinguished the rank and precedence even of those who did succeed in being presented. Some ladies were kissed by the king, others were not; some had to stand, whereas others had the right to sit. The baronne d'Oberkampf on being presented to Louis XVI was not offered a seat, but "la duchesse de la Vrillière qui me présentait s'assit pour un moment sur le tabouret, en présence de la reine, car elle avait droit à cet honneur."[60] In the course of the eighteenth century the restrictions governing presentation at court were applied more severely than in the past. But even to the old nobility, the commercial spirit was not strange. Tighter restrictions on the *honneurs de la cour* increased the market value of some titles. In 1763 Jean-Nicolas Beaujour, the royal genealogist, drew the king's attention to the numbers of noblemen desiring to enjoy their right to this honor: "il est devenu la source des fortunes les plus considérables par les mariages avantageux qu'il procure à ceux qui en sont suscep- tibles."[61] Many poorer noblemen, hopeful of bettering their own fortunes or those of their children by marriage, traveled at great expense from the provinces to Versailles in order to be presented and so to prove the anti- quity of their lineage.

The new aristocracy of the eighteenth century was not very con- cerned, however, with the nice distinctions that were made at Versailles. Since before the death of Louis XIV the center of social and cultural life had shifted from Versailles to Paris, from the court of the monarch to the glittering gatherings in the salons of wealthy bourgeois or *anoblis* and their wives.

The nobility of the last century of the ancien régime was thus a far cry from that of the Middle Ages. It included within a single formal cate- gory elements drawn from the ranks of the successful over a period of more than 400 years, in the course of which the kind of activity that brought success had gone through many changes.

Above all, it was as divided economically as the rest of society, so that at the end of the century the Girondist Brissot could claim that "la noblesse pauvre, cette nombreuse classe de gentilshommes cultivateurs, bornée par un préjugé gothique à un seul état" was the most pitiful "vic- time du despotisme et de l'aristocratie des grands et des riches."[62] Perhaps the term aristocracy, which Brissot used in this passage, describes the class we have been discussing better than the term nobility. The latter suggests a closed caste and long descent by blood from noble ancestors, whereas the former suggests rather a social, cultural, and economic distinction. Turgot may have been exaggerating somewhat when he declared in 1776 that the *corps des nobles* enjoying tax exemptions included "tout le corps des riches" and that "la cause des privilégiés est devenue la cause du riche contre le pauvre." There were after all plenty of poor nobles and their cause was not quite that of the rich. But the great statesman's association of aristocracy and wealth is worth bearing in mind.

## THE *TIERS*

### The Bourgeoisie

A slight improvement on the tiers as a social category, the bourgeoisie still remains a large and ill-defined social group, covering a wide range of social and economic interests, which were often in conflict with one another.[63] As a whole, to judge by a recent investigation of eighteenth-century Paris,[64] it was less wealthy than the court nobility; but among the top people in the bourgeoisie—merchant-bankers, merchant-industrialists, and above all financiers (the most powerful of all and closest to the government)—there were fortunes rivaling and surpassing those of the nobility. Yet those "top people" are not always appropriately described as bourgeois. Many had entered the ranks of the aristocracy. At its summit, therefore, the bourgeoisie shaded off into the aristocracy; at its base it shaded off into the peuple.[65] Some of the richest men in the bourgeoisie were connected with the trade and commerce of port towns such as Rouen, Saint-Malo, Nantes, La Rochelle, Bordeaux, and Marseille. Many of them had strong antimercantilist views and played an important part in promoting reformist and libertarian ideas even in the seventeenth century.[66] At the same time, paradoxically, they developed the slave trade on which, increasingly in the eighteenth century, their fortunes were built. At the end of the seventeenth century the most powerful of them were at once bankers and businessmen. Thomas Le Gendre (1638–1706), for instance, acted as a ship broker, banker, importer, and director of the East India Company. A Huguenot converted to Catholicism after the revocation of the Edict of Nantes, he was able to maintain contacts through Huguenot refugees with merchants in Holland and thus succeeded, despite the war with the English and the Dutch, in arranging shipments of grain on a large scale from Holland and Scandinavia during the famine years of 1693 to 1694.[67] Samuel Bernard, another convert to Catholicism, was likewise able to make good use of members of his family who had chosen to retain their religion and change their nationality: two of his brothers were bankers in Frankfurt and Strasbourg, and two brothers-in-law had banking interests in London and Leipzig. By working with them, Bernard could gather together considerable capital when money was scarce, and the government frequently came to him cap in hand. Bernard also made a fortune supplying the navy with stores from northern and central Europe and by 1696 he was given a monopoly of this traffic. He and Le Gendre were among the few people at the time with sufficient capital to buy up the prizes of the French privateers and this activity brought in huge profits. Some other merchants and ship brokers in Nantes, Saint-Malo, and La Rochelle also did well out of privateering; and it seems likely that the profits from this activity provided the capital for the lucrative slave trade on which the Atlantic port towns grew wealthy in the eighteenth century.

In the course of the eighteenth century—between 1716 and 1770—the overseas trade of France tripled. Above all, it was cotton, sugar, and slaves that enriched and multiplied the merchants of France.[68] Some 600 ships plied the golden triangle from France to West Africa, to the West Indies and back to France again. Miscellaneous articles were carried to

West Africa to be exchanged for slaves; the slaves were shipped to Santo Domingo, where they were used to purchase sugar, and the sugar was then transported back to France to be refined in the new refineries around Nantes.[69] This trade with the West Indies has been set at about one-sixth of the entire commerce of France in the eighteenth century[70] and it was hugely profitable. During the period preceding the Revolution French exports to West Africa totaled 18 million livres, whereas imports were only 100,000 livres. Imports from the West Indies into France, on the other hand, were valued at 185 million livres, but exports totaled less than 78 million livres. The missing link, of course, is provided by the slaves. Raynal and Labedat estimate that some 23,520 were shipped to the West Indies in the year 1769 alone.[71] The fortunes of the great merchant families of Bordeaux, Saint-Malo, and particularly Nantes—the Montaudouins, the Wailshes, the Bouteillers, as well as lesser people who invested in their undertakings—were thus built, ultimately, on the slave trade. The importance of the trade can be measured by the fact that in 1763 when the Treaty of Paris was being drawn up, the French negotiators were especially anxious to recover Martinique and Guadeloupe. Sixty thousand French colonists in Canada were sacrificed gaily to the West Indies trade, to the united applause of the bourgeoisie and the philosophes. Voltaire's famous remark about the "quelques arpents de neige" in Canada reflects the position of the commercial and financial interests that were predominant in the circle of Madame de Pompadour and her friend, the great financier Pâris Duverney.

The most successful and opulent of the merchants—we have already mentioned the Bernards and the Crozats—entered the world of finance, or court capitalism, the topmost echelon of the bourgeoisie of the ancien régime.[72] These men were very wealthy indeed. Allowing for exaggeration, we can get some idea of their wealth from the dowries they were said to have given their daughters. La Live de Bellegarde is supposed to have given each of his daughters 300,000 livres in cash and 10,000 livres worth of jewelry. Antoine Crozat gave one of his daughters a million and a half, together with 50,000 livres for her mother-in-law, the duchesse de Bouillon. The daughter of Samuel Bernard brought a dowry of a million when she married the son of Président Môlé.[73]

One of the best times for the financiers was the administration of Cardinal Fleury (1726–43), which saw the definitive organization of the *ferme générale* with the *bail* (lease) Carlier in 1726. The ferme générale was a syndicate of financiers who bought from the government, in return for a guaranteed prepaid sum, the right to collect all the indirect taxes (salt, tobacco, wine and spirits, various duties levied at the frontiers of the state and of provinces, tolls on goods entering Paris, and so on). These might of course yield more or less than the amount guaranteed to the government, depending on the vigor and efficiency with which they were collected and on the attitude of the government to the *fermiers*. In general, they yielded considerably more. "Ce fut en effet une exploitation éhontée, que ce bail Carlier, inférieur d'une dizaine de millions peut-être au prix qui eût dû être obtenu," writes Marcel Marion, an authority on the history of French finance.[74] There is no doubt, Marion adds, that many fortunes were built on this bail Carlier and on the bail Bourgeois which was granted to the same tax farmers to collect taxes still outstanding for the period from 1721 to 1726.

Naturally, the wealth of the financiers and *fermiers-généraux* provoked resentment and envy among almost all classes of the population, those from which they emerged as well as those that they overtook. Moreover, the agents of the fermiers were hated by both peasants and landlords, for whatever the fermiers got out of the peasants left that much less for the landlords. This helps to explain why the parlements, which were closely allied with the landed interests, took the lead in harassing the fermiers and their agents at every turn, even taking the part of obvious swindlers and smugglers.[75]

Disliked by almost everybody, the financiers were the butt of a great deal of satire. But the unflattering portraits drawn of them by countless writers, including Boileau, Regnard, and especially Le Sage (in his comedy *Turcaret*) tell us—at best—more about what people thought or wanted to think of them than about what they were. Some did rise from very humble circumstances to great wealth. Pâris Duverney, the true ruler of France during the Regency, according to Président Hénault,[76] was the son of an innkeeper. But others came from respectable bourgeois families and their careers were not unduly shady. Bouret began as a *receveur général* at La Rochelle, Dupin was the son of a *receveur des tailles*. Others, such as Lallemant de Retz, La Live de Bellegarde and d'Arnoncourt, fermiers généraux in 1726, belonged to comfortably off and well-respected families. After the mid-century particularly, the tax farmers were drawn from the cream of the bourgeoisie and there was hardly a Turcaret among them; Lavoisier, the chemist, and Benjamin de La Borde, the musicologist, both tax farmers in the second half of the century, were conscientious and distinguished men by any standard.

In the eighteenth century the ferme was in fact a business enterprise that demanded capital, skill, and even a certain integrity from those who took part in it. Large numbers of people were involved in its operations. Many of the sixty farmers—forty after 1780—themselves borrowed the money to purchase their place in the lease and shares were often split two or three ways with other financiers. The number of persons employed by the ferme totaled 30,000 in the late eighteenth century and in Paris alone it occupied several great offices. The fermiers themselves directed the enter-

prise: each served on several committees—for accounts, tobacco, personnel, litigation, and so on—through which the ferme was administered, and
each had to go on periodic tours of inspection into the country. Moreover,
in the second half of the century the fermiers seem not to have made
unreasonable profits. Their expenses were high and, partly as a result of
the very efficiency with which they worked, the cost of the lease kept rising.
A 4 to 6 percent return on investment seems to have been usual in the
period from 1756 to 1780.[77]

Not only was the ferme a vast and highly organized business enterprise involving both the wealthiest members of the bourgeoisie and a whole
army of bureaucrats and *commis,* it was closely connected with the government and the court, who could not do without it. Even in 1716 when a
*chambre de justice* was set up to look into suspected irregularities in the
activities of the financiers, the government did not pursue its prey very
vigorously. The wealthiest were permitted to buy themselves out of trouble
with large gifts to the treasury (Hénault is said to have handed over 4
million and Bernard 10 million). The principal victims of this investigation
seem to have been the smaller fry of agents and receveurs, who, being
directly in contact with the population, attracted a good deal of unpopularity. The fermiers were also linked to the court through the marriages of
wealthy *filles de finance* to the sons of noblemen and eminent robins. "La
dot de presque toutes les épouses des seigneurs est sortie de la caisse des
fermes," Mercier declared.[78]

Moreover, the ferme was a direct source of revenue for members of
the government, courtiers, and the royal family itself. The comptroller
general of finance got a handout, with the signing of each six-year lease, of
up to 300,000 livres. Another 24,000 was paid to the contractor general,
the straw man in whose name the lease was drawn up with the comptroller-
general, and this often went to a favorite of the latter. In addition, many
of the places in the ferme were burdened with provisions for emoluments
for favorites—fifty-five out of sixty supposedly when the Abbé Terray was
comptroller general. A clerical indiscretion in 1774 revealed that about
400,000 was paid out in pensions of one kind or another and that the
beneficiaries included members of the royal family. The nobility and the
king himself also invested directly in the ferme, using a front man to conceal their participation.[79]

In the last century of the ancien régime the great *bourgeoisie de
finance* thus occupied a central place in the state, being intimately related
to the court, the government, and the nobility itself. Its rise to power and
influence was symbolized by the elevation of Madame de Pompadour, who
was herself connected with the world of finance, to the position of official
mistress of Louis XV.

Though the financiers adopted many of the manners of the court and the nobility, they also helped to propagate ways of thinking that were different from those of the court and the nobility. Before the gaze of the financier all essences and qualities dissolved into measurable quantities. Everything had its price. When the duchesse de la Vrillière made the gesture of sitting down briefly in the presence of the queen, she was both confirming and having confirmed a particular status by which she, as a person, was defined. To the financiers, on the other hand, this court etiquette was an empty mummery. Not unnaturally, the demystification of traditional social, religious, and aesthetic ideas and values undertaken by the writers and thinkers of the eighteenth century found a receptive audience among the financiers. They were, in fact, numerous among the supporters of the *Modernes* in the famous *Querelle* and some of them made really significant personal contributions to the new study of man and his institutions and of the natural world. Helvétius and Lavoisier, both fermiers généraux, were important figures in the intellectual life of the eighteenth century. As patrons of literature and the arts the financiers were unmatched. It was the wealthy bourgeoisie of finance rather than the court that in the eighteenth century employed architects, painters, sculptors, and musicians. It was their love of pleasure, their worldliness, their frank, even cynical, outlook that artists of the age returned to them, transformed into stone, oils, or sound. A whole luxury industry of jewelers, goldsmiths, mirror makers, furniture makers, was spawned to meet the demands of the new tone setters. Among the patrons of literature in the eighteenth century some of the best-known belonged to the world of finance: the Dupins who took up the young Jean-Jacques, the d'Épinays who were associated for years with Diderot and Grimm, the *salonnières*—Madame Doublet de Persan, Madame Geoffrin, Madame Du Boccage, Madame Necker, to mention but a few. Helvétius himself was generous to many men of letters. At the home of Le Riche de La Poupelinière the most celebrated figures in the musical world gathered to discuss their art and to hear trial performances of new works by both Frenchmen and foreigners.

Reformers, philosophes or supporters of the philosophes, patrons of the arts, the bourgeoisie de finance had assumed something very like the cultural leadership of France in the eighteenth century. Yet it was by no means popular. It was hated by the peasantry and all the less-wealthy citizens, envied and resented by a good part of the nobility, and regarded with suspicion even by those merchants in the ports and the provincial towns from whose ranks many of the financiers themselves had risen. In general, writes one historian, the merchants "distrusted the financiers, whom they considered court favorites and parasites, and the speculators, whom they thought dangerous and immoral. They believed, perhaps correctly, that capitalism at Paris weakened public credit, milked the royal treasury, raised the interest rate, and threatened the entire business world with a credit crisis and chain reactions of bankruptcies."[80] It may not be an accident that certain "bourgeois" forms of literature, like the *drame,* which were poorly received in Paris, succeeded in the provinces. The position of the brilliant and cultured financier class was in fact ambiguous, for they lived off the rational exploitation of what was increasingly felt to be an irrational and iniquitous social system. They were, in Sombart's pithy phrase, "Fettaugen auf der Suppe"—little beads of fat on the top of the soup.[81]

Of the provincial merchants who looked askance at the wealthy and extravagant financial circles of Paris, many were *marchands-fabricants;* their business was not heady speculation, but the production and exchange of goods. Industry in eighteenth-century France was not, on the whole, concentrated and urban, as in the nineteenth century, but dispersed in the country, and its earliest capitalist forms were based on the merchant, rather than on the old-style guild craftsman, who was bound to the town, to traditional markets, sources of labor, and methods of work. The merchants supplied the raw materials—wool or flax—to workers scattered over the countryside. The peasants, for their part, were glad to get the work, since few of them had enough land to live by. Cottage industries were in fact encouraged by the government as a means of alleviating rural distress without having to effect any far-reaching reforms.

The numbers employed in the putting-out industries were considerable. The lace industry alone employed 17,300 workers in 1669.[82] The rural communities around Saint-Quentin are said to have supplied some 2,000 weavers and 25,000 spinners.[83] In a few places there were significant concentrations of working people, as at the big Van Robais mills at Abbeville, which employed about 1,500 workers, or at Louviers, Sedan, Elbeuf and Reims.[84] The directors of these enterprises were often rich enough to pass into the nobility, but they were less numerous than the *maîtres-marchands* or marchands-fabricants.

In general, there was no industry in a modern sense in eighteenth-century France. By 1790, when England had already 200 spinning mills equipped with 7,000 to 8,000 Arkwright machines, there were no more than 8 in all of France.[85] The French government tried to remedy this situation by importing the new machines and sending over agents to learn the new techniques and to entice English workers to France, but its efforts were not notably successful.[86]

Wealthy bourgeois involved in manufacturing in the eighteenth century were thus first and foremost tradesmen. Characteristically, capitalist undertakings in France in the eighteenth century—outside of agriculture—involved very few fixed assets or investments. Companies were often set up for a particular purpose and then disbanded; what continuity there was in

business history was in persons or families rather than in firms. Even business premises were rented rather than owned. Overseas merchants viewed
each voyage as a single venture. At the end of the trip the vessel would
be sold and the loss or gain from this transaction entered into the profit
or loss of the undertaking as a whole. Likewise the marchands-fabricants
had few or no fixed assets. In eighteenth-century books of accounts and
accounting treatises the concept of depreciation costs and reserves is
unknown.[87] There was thus a considerable amount of improvisation, skill,
and personal decision making in the conduct of business and industry in
the eighteenth century. The successful bourgeois could well identify himself
with his agile wit and his nose for affairs rather than, as the nobleman
might do, with a fixed station in society, or as the later industrialist was to
do with his "works," the factory he had built, the goods he had produced,
the town he controlled.

Below the thin top layer of international merchants, marchands-
fabricants, merchant-bankers, and financiers stood a number of groups of
varying size and economic importance, all belonging to the bourgeoisie:
small tradesmen or master craftsmen, professional men (lawyers, doctors,
teachers, writers, and so on), bureaucrats in the royal administration,
holders of municipal and royal offices, and *rentiers*. These groups formed
the backbone of the bourgeoisie in the ancien régime. Even in a big trading
city and port like Bordeaux what one might call the active entrepreneurial
class was only a minority of the bourgeoisie. In 1789 there were 1,100
officiers, professionals, rentiers, and property owners, as against 700 merchants, brokers, and sugar refiners in the city. At Rouen, a center of industry, banking, and maritime trade, the administrative and judicial officiers,
proprietors, and rentiers outnumbered the merchants and brokers by more
than three to one.[88]
   Let us look briefly at some of the main social groups constituting
the mass of the bourgeoisie.
   Independent tradesmen and craftsmen still made up a substantial
group in the main cities, but most of them occupied the lowest rung on the
bourgeois ladder, both economically and in social prestige. In a recent
study of Parisian society in 1749, based on an analysis of marriage contracts,[89] the majority of the maîtres-marchands—a category that must have
included a variety of persons: artisans with one or two workers, small
wholesalers, the better off retailers—are found to have had fortunes varying
from 500 to 15,000 livres, which places them considerably below the professional classes, the bureaucrats, and the officiers. Nevertheless, compared
to the humblest tradespeople—"petits marchands qui revendent en détail
ce qu'ils ont déjà acheté en détail," as Mercier put it[90]—the maîtres-
marchands were well-to-do and established. These *revendeurs* (sellers of

second-hand goods), *fripiers, herbiers, détaillants de sel,* cannot have been much better off than the working people from whose miserable earnings they eked out their own living.

The elite of the *marchands* was fairly well off. Although only a small percentage of their own group, they constitute a large percentage of a total number of persons found by Daumard and Furet to have had fortunes of between 15,000 and 50,000 livres. And in the course of the eighteenth century their lot may well have improved further. The return of economic prosperity in the eighteenth century brought with it an expansion of the market and led to a growing separation of the maker or producer from the trader and of the wholesaler from the retailer. In the middle of the seventeenth century, for instance, Parisians still bought much of their corn from farmers rather than traders. By the eighteenth century the population of shopkeepers had grown apace.[91] Moreover, there was a significant shift in the organization of the retail trade. The *tapissiers* were the first, it seems, to extend the range of the articles they sold to include items not made by them. In addition to mattresses, curtains, and tapestries, they offered for sale tables, chairs, mirrors, lighting fixtures, even paintings. The storekeeper thus became independent of the craftsman and the guild and organized his business according to the requirements of the consumer rather than of the producer. The owners of the new furniture stores or the new novelty stores for ladies, such as the "Petit Dunkerque" described by Mercier, must have been relatively well-to-do. Contemporary sources indicate that fairly large amounts of capital were needed to set up such retail businesses as mercer's shops, china shops, or even the better class of grocers.[92]

Outside of Paris, to be sure, most tradespeople were still linked to the producer and governed by guild and corporation regulations—jewelers, silversmiths, cutlers such as Denis Diderot's father, watchmakers such as Beaumarchars or the father of Jean-Jacques Rousseau. These were by no means poor or ignorant men. Many were educated and interested in political, economic, and technical matters. Some, such as Romilly, the watchmaker, contributed technical articles to the *Encyclopédie* or advised the editors on matters concerning their speciality. Rarely employing more than two to four *compagnons* or apprentices in their shop, these master craftsmen were coming under increasing pressure, however, from the more capitalistically oriented marchands-fabricants. At Lyons in the course of the eighteenth century, the entire silk industry was completely dominated by the marchands-fabricants and the master craftsmen were reduced to simple workers. Elsewhere they were fighting a last-ditch battle. At Lille the traditional guild-organized industries sought in vain to defend themselves against the marchands-fabricants who were exploiting the labor of the surrounding small towns, such as Roubaix. In Geneva, Romilly, the watchmaker-friend of Rousseau and Diderot, complained of "unfair" competition from the rural workers in the Jura valleys.[93] In 1776 Turgot could already distinguish between the "simples artisans, qui n'ont point d'autre bien que leurs bras, qui n'avancent que leur travail journalier et n'ont de profit que leurs salaires" and the "entrepreneurs manufacturiers, maîtres fabricants, tous possesseurs de gros capitaux, qu'ils font valoir en faisant travailler par le moyen de leurs avances."[94] By the end of the eighteenth century, according to Sée, "les maîtres ouvriers sont animés d'une haine très violente contre les marchands."[95] The seeds of future struggles among the revolutionary parties may perhaps be found here. At all events, the differences within the bourgeoisie between the more capitalistically minded maîtres-marchands or marchands-fabricants and their traditionally oriented brethren with their emphasis on the immediate relation of supply and demand, of producer and client, found an early expression in the conflict within the Enlightenment between Jean-Jacques Rousseau and the main army of the philosophes.

In the professional classes the highest place, both economically and socially, was occupied by doctors and lawyers. Artists and literary men came somewhat lower in the hierarchy, tutors (dancing masters, fencing masters, music teachers, and so on) lower still, while most schoolmasters who were not ecclesiastics may even be more properly ranked among the lower classes.

Though not usually as well-to-do as the upper crust of officeholders and rentiers, the doctors and lawyers were highly regarded on account of their education and ability. Many had excellent libraries, which included the latest productions of the philosophes, and their work kept them abreast of the latest developments—intellectual, scientific, political—in the world at large.[96] Doctors like Camille Falconet and Bordeu were in the van of the freethinking spirits of their time and Diderot could appreciate them both. In some provincial centers the professionals founded new learned and scientific societies, or reading circles; in others, as at Dijon, they wrested control of the old academies from the robe and turned them from their traditional humanist occupations towards politics, agriculture, and science.[97] Moreover, the old bourgeois pride in personal achievement was still strong in these men, together with the traditional bourgeois contempt for those who owed their rank and privileges only to their birth. They must have listened with pleasure to the great chancellor d'Aguesseau when, in an address on the independence of the *avocat* in 1698, he recalled that "those distinctions which are founded only on the accident of birth, those great names which pander to the pride of ordinary men and which dazzle even the wise, become useless accessories in a profession in which virtue alone is the foundation of nobility and men are respected not because of what their fathers did, but because of what they have done themselves."

As he enters his profession, d'Aguesseau declared, the avocat leaves behind him the rank that prejudice assigned to him in the world and assumes the one that reason gives him in the order of nature and truth.[98] It would be hard to express more forcefully the common bourgeois view that although indeed there are and must be distinctions among men, these distinctions should be based on merit and ability, not on birth and inherited rank.

D'Aguesseau's views might also have been shared by some of those bourgeois who were employed in various capacities in the royal administration, in the fermes, and in the intendancies (finance, commerce, and so on), or who were in the service of great noblemen as intendants or administrators of their estates. The wealthiest members of this group seem to have been those who actually owned their posts. "Les officiers et leurs épouses apportent dans la corbeille de noces des fortunes qui révèlent aux plus hauts niveaux, la partie la plus riche du Tiers Etat," according to Daumard and Furet. But even the others figure prominently among the wealthier members of the bourgeoisie.

Second only to the merchants in numbers, in Paris at least, was the large group of rentiers and bourgeois "sans profession," men who signed themselves simply "bourgeois," with no indication of a trade or profession. These people varied widely: "le titre regroupe l'ensemble des rentiers roturiers, de l'usurier au notable de quarter depuis plusieurs générations."[99] Who were they? Retired merchants, retired lawyers and doctors, children of people who had accumulated a little fortune, widows and old maids such as the two Habert sisters in Marivaux's *Paysan Parvenu*. Their incomes varied greatly, more than for any of the groups studied by Daumard and Furet. Some were well-off, with fortunes rising to 500,000 livres. The majority seem to have been fairly modest. Few could afford more than one ill-paid servant for a whole family.[100] There was little love lost between these careful bourgeois and the more adventurous and brilliant *négociants* and financiers, or for that matter, the nobility and the robe. The rentes on which they lived represented income from loans to the state, to the municipalities, to the clergy, to the various *pays d'Etat,* or to private persons. Some of these, like the clergy, were good payers, but then they offered a low rate of return (2–2½ percent).[101] The state, on the other hand, which paid more and offered the investor more scope, was erratic and unreliable, often cutting its rates arbitrarily or cynically forcing repayment of the borrowed money on terms that were disastrous to the lenders. Yet the economy of the ancien régime provided so few outlets for capital that the rentier could not withdraw his support from the state. The government's treatment of him, however, caused a great deal of resentment. On several occasions Colbert cut back incomes from rentes on the grounds that he wanted to encourage capital to flow into commerce and industry. In 1710, 1713, and 1715 there were again "reductions" in the rentes and the severe reductions of the years 1720 to 1723, following on the collapse of Law's *système*, ruined many decent bourgeois families.[102] Colbert's unpopularity in certain sections of the bourgeoisie, which finds expression in the writings of the *Anciens* in particular, may well be due to his treatment of the rentiers, who must have found it galling to compare the success of the financiers and *traitants* with their own reverses. The rentiers got little support from anybody, including the parlements. The Parlement de Paris made some noises of protest, it is true, but the provincial parlements, which represented the great landowners, often suggested simple repudiation of the debts of the state as an alternative to the fiscal reforms that they feared more than anything. The predominantly bourgeois rentier class was thus not a particularly happy one in the last century of the ancien régime. It resented the state's cavalier attitude to those who subscribed to public loans, it envied the wealthy financiers and fermiers-généraux, and it distrusted the aristocracy, both of sword and of robe. It may well be that some of the ideas of Rousseau, for instance,—his hatred of luxury, his attack on finance, his concern with morality, his fear of economic development, his criticisms of despotic government and of aristocracy—found an echo in the hearts not only of old-style craftsmen but of the rentiers in the larger cities of France.

Despite differences among them, the eighteenth-century French bourgeois should probably be distinguished as a group from their nineteenth-century counterparts. Sombart, whose analysis may be more applicable to the French bourgeoisie than to that of England or America, discerns the essence of the old-style bourgeois in his faithfulness to the idea that man is the measure of all things. "In all his thinking and planning, in all his doing and getting done, the determining factor was the weal and the woe of man. . . . All, . . . the great landowner and the great merchant, the banker and the speculator, the manufacturer and the wool merchant, have continued to make their business activity fit the demands of healthy humanity; for all of them business is still a means to the end of life."[103] They value wealth and pursue it eagerly, but it is not an end in itself; it is a means to various human ends—pleasure, beauty, status, society, independence. Indeed, the ultimate goal of the prenineteenth-century bourgeois was to withdraw from affairs and to occupy himself with philosophy, literature, or science.[104]

The very conduct of business was different from that of the nineteenth-century industrial capitalist. The early bourgeois aimed to achieve maximum results with minimum outlay; he still sought his profit, on the whole, by selling at the highest possible price to a limited market, not by selling at the lowest possible price to a mass market. Colbert believed that the population of the world was unchanging; Fontenelle believed the proportion of elite to the *peuple* would remain always fairly steady; likewise, to the early businessman, until fairly late in the eighteenth century at least, the market seemed to be not an expanding one, but a static one. His clientele was circumscribed and he claimed it for his own, just as the nations of Europe tried to monopolize the trade of their colonies. Poaching on your neighbor's clientele, by advertisement, underselling, or cutting out of middlemen was regarded as un-Christian and was forbidden in many city ordinances. Above all, since man was still the measure in a world that remained deeply attached to humanist traditions, the highest goal of all business and industrial activity was decently to supply human wants. Production in itself had not yet become the goal as well as the means of business, and the purely quantitative assessment of the products of trade and industry—in terms not of their human value or use value but of their exchange value—had not yet invaded the whole of man's thinking and feeling life. Finally, technical progress was still frequently subordinated to human well-being. "Si un ouvrage est à un prix médiocre, et qui convienne également à celui qui l'achète et à l'ouvrier qui l'a fait," writes Montesquieu, "les machines qui en simplifieraient la manufacture, c'est-à-dire, qui diminueraient le nombre des ouvriers, seraient pernicieuses."[105] This idea is found not only in the writings of mercantilists like Colbert and Montesquieu, for whom commerce must serve primarily to maintain the existing social structure, but in those of revolutionary social critics such as Rousseau; and it was not strange to businessmen themselves.[106] Ideas and attitudes, even in advanced business circles, did not always change as rapidly as actual practice.

The eighteenth-century bourgeoisie thus remained attached to a certain humanist tradition. Yet, as we have seen, there were tensions within it. The master craftsman or small rentier, for instance, might be fairly conservative, respectful of law and order, often quite pious. He would still maintain the old bourgeois values of prudence, frugality, foresight, charity, "honest" dealings, and "honest" profit.[107] The négociants, the marchands-fabricants, and the financiers, on the other hand, were probably more adventurous and "enlightened"; sometimes, too, more extravagant, pleasure loving, and irreligious. Less bound by old ideas and old techniques, they constantly strained to break down or reduce traditional restrictions and regulations on trade and industry, which the craftsmen, for instance, wished to see maintained.

By the second half of the eighteenth century the tensions within the bourgeoisie began to become serious. The new economists—Cantillon, Hume, Quesnay and the Physiocrats, and finally Adam Smith—propounded doctrines of free trade and expansion. "Value" for the Physiocrats, for instance, was no longer determined by human needs or divine commandments. It expressed a ratio of supply and demand or a capacity for increasing the total wealth of a nation. The accent came to be placed on expanding production and expanding the market, two of the fundamental characteristics of modern capitalist economy, as opposed to the older economy, in which capitalism simply found a corner for itself within an overall feudal framework and the bourgeois occupied a—relatively circumscribed—place in the shadow of noblemen and peasants. Is it an accident that at the same time the notions of novelty and creativity began to assume prominence in the work of writers and scientists, or that the philosophes emerged from the secret societies where they had concealed themselves in the seventeenth and even to some degree in the eighteenth century and progressively broadened the public to which they addressed themselves? The importance of the economic and demographic upsurge of the second half of the eighteenth century, it seems, can hardly be overestimated.

## The Peuple

Overriding the conflict within the bourgeoisie between the older and newer wings was another conflict, separating the thin layer of the bourgeoisie as a whole from the other 90 percent or so of the French population, the peuple, by which was meant in the first instance the countryfolk, but also without doubt the *peuple des villes*, the working class.[108] The distinction between these two groups—the one "enlightened," the other "superstitious," the one law-abiding, the other insubordinate, the one prudent and full of foresight, the other, like Rousseau's savage, living for the day and thoughtless of the morrow, the one diligent and industrious, the other, again like Rousseau's savage, supposedly indolent and working only to satisfy immediate needs—is a constantly recurring theme in thought and literature in the seventeenth and eighteenth centuries.[109] With the founding of the *hôpital-général* in 1657 and the *grand renfermement* of the poor—events that had their counterpart in almost every country to Europe —it became consecrated, as it were, in the law of the land itself. The grand renfermement was a roundup of the poor, of beggars, vagrants, idiots, socially rootless people of all kinds, into institutions where they could be supervised and put to useful work, saved from "la mendicité et l'oisiveté  .  .  .   source de tous les désordres," according the the edict of 1656.[110] As Michel Foucault observes, the purpose of the grand renfermement was double—to absorb the workless and avoid riots, and to provide cheap labor for times when demand was high; above all, it was an attempt by the bourgeoisie, in the name of virtue, law, and order, to impose its values on the rest of society and to control physically those who would not or could not share them. "Les murs de l'internement enferment en quelque sorte le négatif de cette cité morale, dont la conscience bourgeoise commence à rêver au XVII<sup>e</sup> siècle  .  .  .  Dans l'ombre de la cité bourgeoise, naît cette étrange république du bien qu'on impose de force à tous ceux qu'on soupçonne d'appartenir au mal."[111] Thus in 1662 and again in 1669 Colbert prohibited the giving of alms outside churches, the sheltering of vagabonds, and the feeding of the indigent. The 40,000 or 50,000 beggars of Paris were to be put to work by the hôpital-général. "Les manufactures des hôpitaux," Colbert declared, "doivent être partout encouragées. Il n'y a rien qui soit plus important pour bannir la fainéantise et l'oisiveté parmi le peuple."[112]

The attitude of the enlightened bourgeoisie to the peuple is again brought into clear focus by the question of slavery. We have seen that the fortunes of the great merchants of the Atlantic ports were built on the slave trade. Thus Montesquieu—a shareholder, incidentally, in the Compagnie des Indes—argued that "l'esclavage est contre nature," but claimed that in some countries it might not be inadmissible. Above all, it was an economic necessity—for the merchants of Nantes, Saint-Malo, and Bordeaux, that is. "Le sucre serait trop cher si l'on ne faisait travailler la plante par des esclaves."[113] "Enlightened" ministers had no other view. "La traite des Noirs," according to Choiseul, "mérite plus de protection que toute autre puisqu'elle est le premier mobile des cultures."[114] "Enlightened" thinkers, pioneers of the new science of economics, supported them. Melon (*Essai politique sur le commerce,* 1734) declared that "L'usage des esclaves, autorisé dans nos colonies, nous apprend que l'esclavage n'est contraire ni à la religion, ni à la morale," and proposed to extend it beyond the colonies. Even the Revolution hesitated to change the regime of slavery. In 1790 the Constituent Assembly heard sympathetically a petition from the merchants of Rouen urging those who were moved by the fate of the black man to heed the voice of "trois millions de Français tremblant pour leurs propriétés, leurs subsistances, et leurs jours."[115]

Many would find a way out similar to that by which the bourgeoisie could justify its handling of the peuple. The Africans were feckless children who had to be forced to work; indeed, they were barely human. "Ceux dont il s'agit sont noirs depuis les pieds jusqu'à la tête," Montesquieu wrote, "et ils ont le nez si écrasé qu'il est presque impossible de les plaindre."[116] Montesquieu's irony is ambiguous. It is not clear enough to establish his practical opposition to the view expressed; it establishes only his inner superiority to it.[117] In other words, while Montesquieu's "enlightment" is reaffirmed, it does not affect his practical acquiescence in the very opinions that it ridicules. To the bourgeois, in short, great champions of natural-law theories, all men were in principle equal. But there was an inevitable practical division, which made it necessary for some to govern others, whether the latter were the "animaux farouches" La Bruyère observed in the fields of France or those that were shipped from Africa to work the sugar plantations of Santo Domingo.

In general, therefore, the distinction in French society between bourgeois and nobleman was real enough and frequently irritating to the bourgeois, but it was by no means as fundamental as might be believed. "There was," as one historian puts it, "between most of the nobility and the proprietary sector of the middle classes, a continuity of investment forms and socioeconomic values that makes them, economically, a single group . . . there were nobles who were capitalists; there were merchants who were nobles. As the proprietary wealth traditionally identified with the aristocracy extended far down into the third estate, so the capitalism traditionally identified with the wealthy third estate penetrated into the second, and into its highest ranks."[118] Within this large group there were many jealousies and rivalries. But they cut across the vague juridical lines separating bourgeois and aristocrat. Mathieu Marais, the bourgeois of Paris, and the die-hard duc de Saint-Simon, for instance, shared an equally fervid hatred of the financier Pâris Duverney.[119] A more profound division in French society in the eighteenth century was probably that between the aristocracy and the bourgeoisie on the one hand and the vast mass of the laboring poor on the other.

The 90 percent or so of Frenchmen who made up the peuple had almost no voice. They did not participate in the culture we know as Enlightenment; perhaps at very best something of what they thought and felt comes through in the writings of Rousseau or of Rétif de La Bretonne, in the sermons of some country priests, in almanacs, collections of songs, jokes, stories or homilies, and other similar publications that do not qualify as "belles lettres"—though mostly even these were made for them, not by them.[120] Yet, like the slaves who are the missing link in the commercial balance between France and her West Indian colonies, the peuple is the unknown silent factor without which we cannot fully grasp the character of the literature, the art, the thought of the eighteenth century. More varied, more free, more critical and questioning than that of the previous age, both in form and in content, the literature of the Enlightenment nonetheless rests on a firm foundation of supposedly universal values. To the vast majority of writers and artists their conception of literature and of culture in general seemed eternal and not subject to question. There was no doubt about what literature was or that it always had been and always would be what it was for them. The confidence and unity of eighteenth-century culture was, however, in all probability largely due to the relative homogeneity of the eighteenth-century public, the hegemony of bourgeois cultural values and, above all, to the very condition of these two factors, the exclusion from the realm of culture, as, indeed, in all but an abstract sense, from that of "humanity," of the people. The traditions of popular culture are foreign and in many ways opposed to those of the humanist bourgeoisie. Nevertheless, this exclusiveness itself casts a shadow from time to time on the smooth surface of eighteenth-century literature. "Anxiety is hidden beneath the illusion of omnipotence," remarks Jean Starobinski, discussing the "black" works of Sade and Beckford.[121] Anxiety about what, if not about those dark forces—psychological, to be sure, but social too—that had been locked away in the hôpitaux, denied, made invisible, kept out or shut in, but that could neither be conjured away nor dispensed with? The literary background of the eighteenth century would be incomplete without some account of the gigantic silent partner in the creation of the culture of the Enlightenment: the peuple.

## WORKERS IN THE TOWNS

The various crafts and trades were subject to two main kinds of regulations, being free, for the most part, only in the country. In the south and center of France and at Lyons, in particular, the system of the *métier réglé* obtained. Here labor was organized in guilds run by the municipality. Entry might be unrestricted or it might be subject to approval by the municipality, but a strict surveillance was maintained over the actual exercise of the craft. In the north and notably in the Paris region the predominant type of guild was the *métier juré,* a strictly hierarchized system that included three types of member: the *maîtres* (the established artisans who ran their own shops), the *compagnons* (their paid workers), and the apprentices (young people learning the trade or craft). The supreme authority in the métier juré was vested in the master craftsmen under the aegis of the king. There was thus less interference by outsiders in methods of production and working conditions, but a far greater exclusiveness and tendency to monopoly. In the sixteenth and seventeenth centuries the royal authority actively favored the métiers jurés, partly no doubt for political reasons (the métiers jurés were directly under its control rather than subject to the municipality), and partly for fiscal reasons (the charter of the métier juré called for regular payments of dues to the crown, for which the leaders of the métier were responsible).

The métier juré thus gradually extended its sway. Certain of its characteristics should be noted. As a public or semipublic institution—not a simple voluntary association—it was in a sense responsible to the community in which it was licensed. It had to serve this community honestly, with products of good quality at a "fair" price. Its products were in fact subject to inspection, and the maître could not—and doubtless would not have wished to—farm out his work to others. He was personally responsible for goods made or sold in his shop. This system of inspection greatly handicapped the urban industries in relation to the rural ones, which were run by the marchands-fabricants and not subject to inspection or organized in guilds, and it aggravated the hostility between the maîtres and the marchands-fabricants. Among the maîtres there was, moreover, a strong feeling of cooperation and brotherhood, which extended to the compagnons where common interests were involved. Both maîtres and compagnons shared a common attitude toward work and society, which found partial expression later in Rousseau's denunciation of "science" and his emphasis on the relation of the worker to the product of his labor, on the social and human significance of work, and on the collective responsibility of the community for each of its members. Maîtres and compagnons alike took a different position on essential social questions from the marchands-fabricants, and it seems clear that the latter, not the former were on the side of progress and "philosophie."

For the compagnons, however, life was often harder than for the maîtres. In principle they were supposed to be able to become master artisans on giving proof of their ability in a *chef d'oeuvre*, or masterpiece, which was judged by a jury of masters or of townspeople. But by the sixteenth century the preparation of the masterpiece had become a costly and lengthy affair, while the various expenses incurred by the new master— the banquet he had to give, his membership dues, and so on—had become extremely onerous. Moreover, many guilds limited the number of masters they were willing to receive, reserving entry to the sons of masters and to those wealthy enough to purchase *lettres de maîtrise*. In one way or another, therefore, the compagnon was excluded from the *maîtrise* and this usually meant being excluded from all the rights of bourgeoisie. The worker had no voting rights, he could not carry arms, and did not mount the guard.[122] Instead of being a stage or grade, his inferiority became a permanent social condition. Thus the number of compagnons continued to rise. Those who tried to help themselves by working clandestinely were severely punished when caught, not only by the maîtres but by the secret societies of the regular compagnons (*compagnonnages*), whose livelihoods were as threatened by these independent workers as those of the master artisans. The compagnonnages were likewise on the watch for *forains* or *alloués,* unqualified outside workers, whom the maître sometimes took on because he could pay them less. Maîtres who engaged in such practices might be struck or boycotted by the compagnonnages.

In general the state lent its support to the maîtres. At the end of the eighteenth century the system by which workers could not leave the *manufactures royales* without written permission of the director was extended to all workers, and a *livret ouvrier* in good order had to be shown by any worker seeking unemployment. Attempts were even made to regiment the workers' leisure, especially in the manufactures royales,

and there were severe punishments for excessive drinking or other "debau-
cheries." Working conditions were not good. The sources vary greatly, but
a working day of twelve to fifteen hours from five in the morning till eight
at night seems to have been not uncommon.[123] By Colbert's time the once
large number of holidays had been reduced to ninety-two. La Fontaine
might cry that "on nous ruine en fêtes" but to the laborer who took his
few pleasures where and when he found them, his concern would have
seemed exaggerated.[124] Wages, on the whole, were very low, though they
varied from trade to trade, and they tended not to get better, since the
state encouraged employers to keep them low in the hope of meeting foreign competition. In bad years the maîtres might not only cut back wages,
they might even try to get rid of their workers. If the harvest was bad and
the price of bread high, the laboring poor would find themselves close to
starvation. In the horrible winter of 1709, for instance, there were bread
riots and looting in Paris, Rouen, and almost all of the provinces.[125]

In the course of the eighteenth century the rise in salaries did not
keep pace with the rise in the cost of living and the working people were
relatively worse off than they had been before. The compagnonnages did
something to improve the worker's lot—one of the reasons for their consistent prohibition throughout the seventeenth and eighteenth centuries
and right into the revolutionary period itself—but they were hamstrung
by their own exclusiveness and internal rivalries.[126] Strikes were frequent.
One source cites five serious instances of labor unrest in the cloth mills at
Sedan between 1712 and 1738.[127] But as action was only local, it was
usually unsuccessful, though in the later eighteenth century more concerted
action occasionally produced results.[128] The government looked on strikes
as rebellions and was prepared to use troops to put them down. The official reports constantly complain of the "esprit de cabale et de mutinerie de
ces ouvriers."[129]

In assessing the life of the working people, however, we should bear
in mind that conditions varied greatly from trade to trade, from region to
region, and from year to year. (This may account in some measure at
least for the enormous divergences among the sources.) Moreover, the
common people did not yet have that sense of time and of regulated living
that was part of the growing culture of capitalism. When they had money,
they spent it gladly in rough fun at the *cabaret* or at the *guinguettes* in the
suburbs. "Le petit peuple," writes Mercier, "danse encore fort et long-
temps; il est le dernier à abandonner les coutumes joyeuses."[130]

In the end there was no class consciousness as we know it today
among the working people.[131] The basic distinction was still very much
that between rich and poor, for if a trade was under pressure the maître
might be almost as poorly off as his compagnons. Indeed, in the course
of the eighteenth century the economic position of the maîtres did decline

continuously and by the end of the century many of them should be probably classed with the workers rather than with the lower bourgeoisie. That
is why during the Revolution the *sans culottes* did not distinguish between
*patrons* and *ouvriers* but between *riches* and *pauvres,* and why the basic
social question was not the organization of labor but the assurance of a
minimum subsistence level.[132]

### THE PEASANTRY

Even more than from the working people of the towns, the thin layer
of nobility and bourgeoisie was separated from the people of the countryside. To the latter, the townsman must often have appeared in the shape
of the enemy—a tax collector, a hard-bargaining merchant, a man of law
to whom large fees had to be paid "for nothing." Even the working people
of the towns paid no direct taxes, except for the capitation which in their
case amounted to very little. The rural worker, on the other hand, was
burdened with tithe and taille. In the country old beliefs and old routines
remained strong. In some areas, indeed, the peasants remained *pagani,*
believing in occult powers, and interpreting Christianity very freely; the
bourgeois, on the other hand, especially the more prosperous bourgeois,
was beginning to characterize himself as the man who had freed himself
from those routines, and even from Christianity, at least as it was understood and practiced in the rural communities.

But just as the bourgeoisie included mutually hostile elements, some
of which were doing well and getting richer, whereas others were doing
poorly and becoming barely distinguishable from the workers, the peasantry was divided within itself. We have seen that a considerable amount
of land in France had come into peasant hands by the eighteenth century.
Those peasants who had enough land of their own to live off—the more
enterprising laboureurs—were relatively wealthy, but they were few in
number and constituted a kind of village aristocracy. In years when grain
was short and fetched high prices they did well while the rest of the working population, urban and rural, suffered. The vast majority of the peasants
held insufficient land of their own. Those who could afford it took out
leases on lands owned by noble or—particularly in the vicinity of the
towns—bourgeois landlords. These leases were renewable, so that the
price could be raised, as it often was, especially in the eighteenth century.
In the south of France and even in Burgundy in the bad time at the end
of the seventeenth century, the system of *métayage* (sharecropping) was
common. Here the peasant paid for the land he leased with a percentage
—from 33-1/3 percent to as much as 50 percent—of his crop. Thus he
was not even able to benefit from periodic increases in the price of grain.
Arthur Young reports that the sharecroppers were very poor and that they

often had to mortgage the entire harvest to come to the seigneur in order to obtain bread.

Many of the poorer peasants added to their income by taking in work from a marchand-fabricant in the nearby town or, if they were luckier, by running a small business, such as an inn. Even so, there were still large numbers of countryfolk who had nothing save the tiniest patch of land and who lived almost entirely by hiring out their labor to the better off farmers. Though not comparable to the dispossessed English peasantry, which had simply become a laboring class with a huge proportion of vagabonds and poor, the number of such *brassiers* in France was high and rising.

The poorer peasants suffered not only the onslaughts of nature—bad harvests, epidemics, high mortality—but the impositions of society. They had constantly to struggle against landlords who tried to make the most of their feudal dues and who encroached on the common lands and pastures of the village. They were harassed by the crown with its ever higher tax demands and other vexations such as the billeting of soldiers. They were exploited by their own better off brethren, who, as tax assessors to the villages, tried to lighten their own burden by exacting as much as possible from the weaker members of the community. "De laboureur à laboureur le plus fort accable le plus faible," Vauban noted.[133]

The misery of the vast mass of the peasantry, particularly at the end of the seventeenth and in the early years of the eighteenth cenutry, was intense and there were frequent uprisings—in 1662 in the Boulonnais, in 1664 in the southwest, in 1670 in the Vivarais, in 1674 in the Bordeaux area, in 1675 in Brittany, in 1703 in Languedoc, in 1706 and 1707 in Périgord and Quercy.[134] The Breton rebels of 1675 formulated their aims: the *Gabelle,* which they took to be a person, was to be shot and killed like a mad dog; all stamped paper—required for legal documents—was to be burned, together with all the acts written upon it; the dovecotes of the seigneurs were to be burned down; the church's tithe was to be abolished; hunting was to be prohibited from March to September; wine to be sold at fixed prices; and tobacco, paid for with the money that had hitherto been soaked up by the taille, to be issued with the holy wafer at Mass! These revolts were ruthlessly suppressed. Six hundred peasants were killed, maimed, or taken prisoner in 1662. In 1675 masses of peasants were hanged. "Les arbres commencent à se pencher sur les grands chemins du poids qu'on leur donne," the duc de Chaulnes, governor of Brittany, wrote.[135] Something of the horror penetrates for a moment into the letters of Madame de Sévigné, who was then residing in her château at Vitré. But only for a moment. "Je trouve tout fort bon," she concludes, "pourvu que les quatre mille hommes de guerre ne m'empêchent pas de me promener dans mes bois qui sont d'une hauteur et d'une beauté merveilleuses."

The eighteenth century was to show more and more concern with the economic aspects of the peasant question and there was also, to be sure, an upsurge of humanitarian feeling. Thus Diderot reminded Helvétius, the wealthy fermier général, for whom "la condition de l'ouvrier . . . est de toutes les conditions peut-être la plus heureuse," of the brutal realities of the laborer's life.[136] Similarly, though he favored the abolition of barriers to trade, as all the philosophes did, Diderot grew indignant at the abstractions of the more doctrinaire champions of liberalism. He had seen famine at Langres and the memory of it haunted him.[137] "Vous n'avez pas la première notion de ce qui se passe dans les temps de disette," he exclaimed.[138] "Vouloir representer une campagne par quatre fermiers aisés, c'est oublier la misère de la multitude."[139]

Yet we should not exaggerate the scope of this humanitarian concern. It was, in some part, dictated by fear. "L'Abbé Galiani craint le peuple," Diderot noted, "et quand il s'agit de pain, il n'y a qu'un homme ivre qui n'en ait pas peur. On voit bien que M. l'Abbé Morellet . . . ne l'a pas vu menacé de la disette dans nos provinces."[140] To Diderot, bourgeois of Paris and of Langres, where he was proud of being a landowner, the peuple was, after all, still the monster to be assuaged. "Le peuple," he declared, "n'est point aimable";[141] it is always ready to rise up in anarchy and destroy the establishments of the propertied. "Dans les émeutes populaires on dirait que chacun est souverain, et s'arroge le droit de vie et de mort."[142] And yet, as Roland Mortier recalled recently,[143] Diderot was far more sympathetic to the common people than many of his contemporaries.

Rousseau, of all the philosophes the closest to the *petit peuple,* argued in *La Nouvelle Héloïse* that education was unnecessary for the peasant and could only disrupt the order of society. And this traditional attitude was shared by most people at the time, including many "reformers."[144] It was La Chalotais who declared, in a plan to reform the educational system of France, that "le bien de la société demande que les connaissances du peuple ne s'étendent pas plus loin que ses occupations."[145] The system introduced by the Revolution and maintained to the present day is indeed one that favors the bourgeoisie; the working classes and the peasants are largely excluded from higher education.

It is important to bear in mind that the culture of the Enlightenment was a minority culture. And this is not simply a curious fact that the student of literature and ideas can put aside when he comes face to face with the texts. The Enlightenment presented itself in universal terms, but the concrete reality in which it was embedded was the struggle of one minority social group to wrest power from another minority social group. The relation of nearly all the Enlighteners to the existing order was thus ambivalent. They criticized what they saw as a growing gap between "rational" political theory and the reality of their society, and they invoked universal principles to question those aspects of their society that were an obstacle to "progress," but it was the progress of the bourgeoisie that they had in mind, whether they knew it or not. They did not envisage, on the whole, an end to minority rule or minority culture as such. Government for them meant government along the lines favored by and favorable to the bourgeoisie, and it was this kind of government that they held to be "rational" or "natural." Culture itself was identified, on the whole, with the culture of the bourgeoisie and it too was taken to be universal. There is not much place in eighteenth-century theory or practice for the old popular culture, though at important moments both Diderot and Rousseau (the former in his posthumously published works and in his reflections on the arts of antiquity in the *Essai sur la peinture,* the latter most notably by his interest in the *fête* as opposed to the classical form of the play) show an unusual awareness of it and a sense of the isolation and even alienation of their own humanist culture.

## NOTES

1. Contemporary estimates vary. Lavoisier calculated that a third of the population of France lived in towns. Arthur Young suggested a fifth. The first census shows that as late as 1846 only 8.6 million Frenchmen lived in towns as against 26.7 million in the country. Reinhard believes that 4 million out of 28 million is a fair estimate of the population that lived in towns of more than 2,000 inhabitants at the end of the eighteenth century [Marcel Reinhard, *Histoire de la population mondiale de 1700 à 1948* (Paris: Editions Montchrestien S.A.R.L., 1949), p. 95; see also Louis Henry, "The population of France in the eighteenth century," in D. V. Glass and D. E. C. Eversley, *Population in History: Essays in Historical Demography* (London: E. J. Arnold & Son Ltd., 1965), pp. 434–56].
2. Reinhard, *Population de 1700 à 1948,* p. 62; see also the table in Reinhard and Armengaud, *Histoire générale de la population mondiale* (Paris: Editions Montchrestien S.A.R.L., 1961), p. 197.
3. Maxime Kovalewsky, *La France économique et sociale à la veille de la Révolution,* 2 vols. (Paris: V. Giard et E. Brière, 1909–11), 1, 116–17.
4. See Bernhard Groethuysen, *Die Entstehung der bürgerlichen Welt- und Lebensanschauung in Frankreich* (Tübingen: Max Niemeyer Verlag, 1927–30).
5. E. J. Hobsbawm, *The Age of Revolution, 1787–1848* (New York: The New American Library Inc., 1962), pp. 33–36; also Reinhard, *Population de 1700 à 1948,* p. 64.
6. Kovalewsky, *La France économique,* 1, 153–54, 309–16 *et passim;* Georges Lefebvre, "Répartition de la propriété et de l'exploitation foncières à la fin de l'ancien régime" and "La Révolution française et les paysans" in his *Études sur la Révolution française* (Paris: Presses Universitaires de France, 1963), pp. 279–

306, 338–67; George V. Taylor, "Non-capitalist wealth and the origins of the French Revolution," *American Historical Review,* 72 (1967), 469–96.

7. On the family structure, see the standard work by Philippe Ariès, *L'Enfant et la vie familiale sous l'Ancien Régime* (Paris: Librairie Plon S.A., 1960), and some excellent pages in Georges Snyders, *La Pédagogie en France aux XVII<sup>e</sup> et XVIII<sup>e</sup> siècles* (Paris: Presses Universitaires de France, 1965), pp. 215–342.

8. Reinhard, *Population de 1700 à 1948,* p. 75. See also Joseph J. Spengler, *France Faces Depopulation* (Durham, N.C.: Duke University Press, 1938), pp. 15–20.

9. Quoted by Régine Pernoud, *Histoire de la bourgeoisie en France,* 2, *Les Temps modernes* (Paris: Editions du Seuil, 1962), 124.

10. Reinhard, *Population de 1700 à 1948,* p. 71; also Robert Mandrou, *La France aux XVII<sup>e</sup> et XVIII<sup>e</sup> siècles* (Paris: Presses Universitaires de France, 1967). On fertility during the last century of the ancien régime, see the important observations of Louis Henry in Glass and Eversley, *Population in History,* pp. 435, 448–52: the "natural" fertility rate is not, as is often imagined, one child per annum for each female; fertility rates are, moreover, determined by sexual mores, age at marriage, and the life cycle of the female.

11. Reinhard, *Population de 1700 à 1948,* pp. 71–74; Henry, in Glass and Eversley, *Population in History*; L. Dubois and F. Dutacq in A. Kleinclausz, ed., *Histoire de Lyon,* 2, *De 1595 à 1814* (Lyons: Librairie Pierre Masson, 1948), 179; Pierre Goubert, "Recent Theories and Research in French Population between 1500 and 1700," in Glass and Eversley, *Population in History,* pp. 457–73. The pessimistic claim of the author of the *Encyclopédie* article "Homme" that "il en meurt plus d'un quart dans la première année, plus d'un tiers en deux ans et au moins la moitié dans les trois premières années" seems not so wide of the mark.

12. Early studies made on parish registers for the periods from 1686 to 1690 and from 1786 to 1790 show a marked increase in the number of persons able to sign their names, especially in the north and east of France. In particularly favored regions illiteracy had dropped to about 25 percent. These findings, first published in 1880 by the French Ministry of Education (*Statistique comparée de l'enseignement primaire 1829–1877*) and reproduced by Carlo Cipolla in his recent *Literacy and Development in the West* (Baltimore: Penguin Books, Inc., 1969, pp. 20–22), have been born out by the work of local historians [for example, Marcel Duval for the area of Carentan in "A travers la Normandie des XVII<sup>e</sup> et XVIII<sup>e</sup> siècles," *Cahiers des Annales de Normandie,* 3 (Caen, 1963), 226]. Nevertheless, as Cipolla emphasizes, literacy is not an abstract achivement. There are degrees of literacy, and being able to write is only one factor in a much vaster complex. The complaint by the author of *De l'Éducation publique* (Amsterdam, 1762), sometimes attributed to Diderot, that 92 percent of French boys received only the most rudimentary schooling or none at all is not to be lightly dismissed.

13. See Werner Sombart, *Luxus und Kapitalismus,* (Berlin: Duncker & Humblot, 1913); also E. J. Hobsbawm, "The Crisis of the Seventeenth Century," in Trevor Aston, ed. *Crisis in Europe, 1560–1660* (Garden City, N. Y.: Doubleday & Co., Inc., 1967), pp. 5–62.

14. It has been pointed out that the term feudal is ambiguous at best and that seigneurial would more aptly describe eighteenth-century conditions [see Alfred Cobban, *The Social Interpretation of the French Revolution* (London: Cambridge University Press, 1965)]. Some French historians have, however, de-

fended the use of the term [see Guy Lemarchand, "Le XVII<sup>e</sup> siècle en France: orientations de recherches nouvelles," *La Pensée*, 138 (1968), 85–108].

15. Boris Porshnev, *Les Soulèvements populaires en France de 1623 à 1648* (Paris: Service d'Edition et de Vente des Productions de l'Education Nationale, 1963)—originally published in Russian. Part of the introduction to this important work appeared in English as "The legend of the seventeenth century in French history," *Past and Present*, 8 (1955), 15–27. On the absolutist state as the instrument of the aristocracy, see also Charles Morazé, *La France bourgeoise, XVIII<sup>e</sup>–XX<sup>e</sup> siècles* (Paris: Librairie Armand Colin, 1946), pp. 66–67. In his book on Turgot, Douglas Dakin concludes that whatever the political parties and factions in England and France did—"whether they concurred in a power being exercised in their interests or whether they opposed a king who was ignoring their demands, their fundamental assumption was always the same: the royal authority exists for a purpose, of which their own wants and desires were the most essential part. The fundamental interests of the aristocracy were never seriously violated in France or in England" [Douglas Dakin, *Turgot and the Ancient Régime in France* (London: Methuen & Co. Ltd., 1939), p. 23].

16. See Lemarchand, "Le XVII<sup>e</sup> siècle en France."

17. See Lefebvre, "Répartition de la propriété" and "La Révolution française et les paysans"; also Henri Sée, *La France économique et sociale au XVIII<sup>e</sup> siècle* (Paris, Librairie Armand Colin, 1925).

18. Kovalewsky, *La France économique*, 1, 132. Kovalewsky exaggerates, however; see Lefebvre, "La Révolution française et les paysans," p. 353.

19. Kovalewsky, *La France économique*, 1, 222–67, gives a useful account of these various sources of income. See also Sée, *La France économique et sociale*, pp. 24–27; Lefebvre, "La Révolution française et les paysans," p. 351; and Albert Colombet, *Les Parlementaires bourguignons à la fin du XVIII<sup>e</sup> siècle* (Lyons: Bosc Frères, M. & L. Riou, 1936), pp. 165–68.

20. Kovalewsky, *La France économique*, 1, 147–48; Lefebvre, "La Révolution française et les paysans," pp. 347–48.

21. George V. Taylor, "Types of capitalism in eighteenth-century France," *English Historical Review*, 79 (1964), 478–97, argues that capitalism in France in the eighteenth century was predominantly proprietary rather than entrepreneurial. The distinction he makes is important. I am less concerned here, however, to distinguish between types of capitalism than to suggest some values and behavior patterns that may be common to most types of capitalist as opposed to feudal or corporative relations.

22. Kovalewsky, *La France économique*, 1, 68–71, 115–19, 360–61, 383. The passage from Necker, *De l'Administration des finances,* is quoted on pp. 360–61. (Translation mine—L. G.)

23. *De l'Administration provinciale et de la réforme de l'impôt,* quoted by Kovalewsky, *La France économique*, 1, 371.

24. In 1784 Necker reckoned that one-third of the prison population was made up of smugglers. Each year, he claimed, 2,300 men, 1,800 women, and 6,000 children are arrested for illegal transportation of salt (*De l'Administration des finance,* quoted by Kovalewsky, *La France économique*, 1, 382–83).

25. Sée, *La France économique et sociale*, p. 7.

26. *Itinerarium Galliae Narbonensis*, 1606, quoted by Albert Babeau, *Les Artisans et domestiques d'autrefois* (Paris: Firmin-Didot Etude, 1886), p. iii.

27. Sée, *La France économique et sociale*, pp. 60–64, Kovalewsky, *La France économique*, 1, 112–14. It should be noted, however, that the parish priest was

not always poor. He might be relatively well-off compared to the rest of the rural population and closer to the comfortable peasant proprietor or to the successful fermier; see Paul Levillot, "Curés campagnards et pratique religieuse," *Annales: Economies, Sociétés, Civilisations,* 11 (1956), 503–4.

28. Kovalewsky, *La France économique,* 1, 114, 295–96; Sée, *La France économique et sociale,* pp. 64–68; E. Préclin, *Le Jansénisme du XVIII<sup>e</sup> siècle et la Constitution Civile du clergé* (Paris: J. Gamber, 1928); abbé A. Sicard, *L'ancien Clergé de France,* 5th ed. (Paris: V. Lecoffre, 1912), 1, 309; see Duval, "L'Election de Carentan du milieu du XVII<sup>e</sup> au milieu du XVIII<sup>e</sup> siècle" in "A travers la Normandie," *Cahiers des Annales de Normandie,* 3, for a detailed and richly documented account of the life of the parish priest in one small area and his relation to the peasantry he served.

29. Quoted by Reinhard, *Population de 1700 à 1948,* p. 101.

30. On the merging of the interests of the two groups within the aristocracy in the eighteenth century, see Philippe Sagnac, *La Formation de la société française moderne,* 2, *La Révolution des idées et des moeurs et le déclin de l'ancien régime* (Paris: Presses Universitaires de France, 1946), 168–69; Sée, *La France économique et sociale,* p. 94; and especially Franklin Ford, *Robe and Sword: the Regrouping of the French aristocracy after Louis XIV* (Cambridge, Mass.: Harvard University Press, 1953). Many sons of magistrates showed no inclination to follow their fathers' careers and preferred the social and intellectual life of the salons. Pont-de-Veyle, the writer and lifelong friend of Madame du Deffand was the eldest son of the President de Ferriol; the witty Bachaumont who presided over a salon with his friend Madame Doublet was also a magistrate's son.

31. On *noblesse par prescription*—that is, basically, by purchase of noble lands, see Jean-Richard Bloch, *L'Anoblissement en France au temps de François 1<sup>er</sup>: essai d'une définition de la condition juridique et sociale de la noblesse au début du XVI<sup>e</sup> siècle* (Paris: Felix Alcan, 1934), pp. 27–61. According to Bloch (pp. 30–31, 73–74), the number of roturiers who slipped into the nobility by this means is not easy to measure. Bloch points out, however, that in the case of persons ennobled by royal letters the total number is much larger than the number of actual letters issued, since it must include the wives and children of the recipients.

32. See Norman Hampson, *A Social History of the French Revolution* (London: Routledge & Kegan Paul Ltd., 1963).

33. Kovalewsky, *La France économique,* 1, 7–10, 297–98. Chateaubriand's description of the daily life of the petty nobility of Brittany in his *Mémoires d'outre-tombe* seems fairly reliable.

34. Duval, in *Cahiers des Annales de Normandie,* 3, notes that in the *élection* of Carentan, out of 100 gentilshommes on the capitation rolls of 1701, 17 paid less than 3 livres, 40 between 1 and 50 livres, and only 1 paid as much as 500 livres. These figures are low, even allowing for cheating and deception on the part of the noblemen.

35. Y. M. Berce, "La Noblesse rurale de sud-ouest sous Louis XIII: de la criminalité aux troubles sociaux," *Annales du Midi,* 1964, pp. 41–59.

36. Quoted by Kovalewsky, *La France économique,* 1, 298.

37. Roland Mousnier, *La Vénalité des offices sous Henri IV et Louis XIII* (Rouen: Editions Maugard, 1945), pp. 18–19.

38. Bloch, *L'Anoblissement en France,* pp. 80–81; also Henri Carré, *La Fin des Parlements* (Paris: Librairie Hachette S. A., 1912), pp. 9–10.

39. Regnard acquired the lands and castle of Grillon near Dourdan, to the south of Paris, in 1699. On his life there, see Alexandre Calame, *Regnard, sa vie et son oeuvre* (Paris: Presses Universitaires de France, 1960), pp. 77–91.

40. Mousnier, *Vénalité des offices,* p. 493.

41. Sombart, *Luxus und Kapitalismus,* p. 22; Kovalewsky, *La France économique,* 1, 108.

42. Roland Mousnier, *Histoire générale des civilisations,* 4, *Les XVIᵉ et XVIIᵉ siècles* (Paris: Presses Universitaires de France, 1954), 4. See also E. J. Hobsbawm, "The crisis of the seventeenth century," pp. 5–62, and B. H. Slicher van Bath, *The Agrarian History of Western Europe, 500–1850,* trans. O. Ordish [London: Edward Arnold (Publishers) Ltd., 1963], pp. 206–20.

43. Philippe Sagnac, *La Formation de la société française moderne,* 1, *La Société et la monarchie absolue, 1661–1715* (Paris: Presses Universitaires de France, 1945, 204–9).

44. Quoted by Sombart, *Luxus und Kapitalismus,* p. 23.

45. L. Sebastien Mercier in *Tableau de Paris,* quoted by Sombart, *Luxus und Kapitalismus,* p. 23; see also Sée, *La France économique et sociale,* p. 82.

46. Sagnac, *Formation de la société française,* 1, 211.

47. Colombet, *Les Parlementaires bourguignons,* pp. 68–73; Carré, *La fin des Parlements,* pp. 2–3.

48. Gaston Roupnel, *La Ville et la campagne au XVIIᵉ siècle; essai sur les populations du pays dijonnais* (Paris: E. Leroux, 1922), p. 215.

49. Carré, *La Fin des Parlements,* pp. 5–7; Sagnac, *Formation de la société française,* 1, 211. Charles de Ribbe, *Les Familles et la société en France avant la Révolution* (Paris: J. Albanel, 1873), quotes from the *livre de raison* of a *conseiller* at the Parlement de Provence in 1718: "Je ne désirois pas que mon père me remît la charge de conseiller; elle coûtoit beaucoup, causoit beaucoup de peine et ne rendoit rien" (p. 406).

50. *Journal de Barbier,* September, 1733.

51. Quoted by Sombart, *Luxus und Kapitalismus,* pp. 22–23. The same point was made in countless works concerning the nobility in the seventeenth century (see, for instance, the works of André Favyn and Vulson de la Colombière).

52. Mousnier, *Vénalité des offices,* pp. 495–97; see also G. Ziegler, *At the Court of Versailles* (New York: E. P. Dutton & Co., Inc., 1966).

53. Sagnac, *Formation de la société française,* 1, 209; see also Taylor in *English Historical Review,* 79 (1964), 480–81.

54. See also Taylor, *English Historical Review,* 79 (1964), 482–83, 488–89.

55. On the role of the nobility in industry in the ancien régime, see Germain Martin, *La grande Industrie en France de 1660 à 1715* (Paris: A. Rousseau, 1899); *La grande Industrie en France sous le règne de Louis XV* (Paris: A. Fontemoing, 1900).

56. Pernoud, *Histoire de la bourgeoisie,* p. 208; see also Lefebvre, "Les mines de Littry" in *Études sur la Révolution française* and Werner Sombart, *Der Bourgeois* (Berlin: Duncker & Humblot, 1913), p. 106, where there is a long list of noblemen with coal-mining concessions.

57. According to Bertrand Gille, *Les Origines de la grande industrie métallurgique en France* (Paris: Editions Montchrestien S.A.R.L., 1947), of 601 forge masters of determinable status listed in the royal investigations of 1771 and 1788, 60 percent were noblemen (p. 130, pp. 173–74).

58. On speculation mania, see Sombart, *Der Bourgeois,* pp. 61–68, 115–23. On later speculation in the 1770s and 1780s on government bonds and chartered joint-

stock companies, see Taylor, *English Historical Review*, 79 (1964), 490–91.

59. It has been estimated that of 942 families presented at court between 1715 and 1790 only 462 would have been able to present proof of unbroken nobility dating back to 1400. But even 520 "interlopers" out of the vast aristocracy of the eighteenth century is small fry indeed (see F. Bluche, "Les Honneurs de la Cour," *Les Cahiers Nobles*, 10–11 [Paris, 1957]).

60. *Mémoires*, quoted by Kovalewsky, *La France économique*, 1, 111.

61. Quoted by Bluche, "Les Honneurs de la Cour."

62. Quoted by Sée, *La France économique et sociale*, pp. 86–87.

63. For an excellent survey, see Albert Soboul, *La France à la veille de la Révolution*, new ed. (Paris: Société d'Editions d'Enseignement Supérieur, 1966), pp. 115–38. There is an illuminating survey of the bourgeoisie in one town in Jeffry Kaplow, *Elbeuf during the Revolutionary Period: History and Social Structure* (Baltimore: The Johns Hopkins Press, 1964), pp. 57–99.

64. A. Daumard and F. Furet, *Structures et relations sociales à Paris au milieu du XVIIIᵉ siècle, Cahiers des Annales*, 18 (Paris: Librairie Armand Colin, 1961).

65. At the conclusion of his study of the nobility under François 1ᵉʳ J. R. Bloch wrote that "il n'y a pas plus de frontière fixe entre les classes qu'il n'y en a entre les provinces. . . Toute une population limitrophe campait désormais sur les confins formant entre les deux ordres une sorte de marche intermédiaire;— monde qui sortait du peuple et n'en était plus, qui tendait vers la noblesse et ne lui appartenait pas encore en entier. C'est lui qui, se couvrant du nom de Tiers Etat, va rejeter la grosse masse paysanne et ouvrière dans la situation misérable d'un Quart Ordre sans traditions, sans droits, sans pouvoirs, sans protecteurs" (*L'Anoblissement en France*, pp. 215–16).

66. See Lionel Rothkrug, *Opposition to Louis XIV: the political and social origins of the French Enlightenment* (Princeton, N. J.: Princeton University Press, 1965), pp. 392–419.

67. Rothkrug, *Opposition to Louis XIV*, pp. 399–400; see also Sagnac, *Formation de la société française*, 1, 205.

68. Sagnac, *Formation de la société française*, 2, 61–62; see also Hobsbawm, "Crisis of the seventeenth century," pp. 53–56. Hobsbawm argues that the development of plantation economies in the European colonies was the most important impetus to domestic trade and manufacturing in seventeenth- and eighteenth-century Europe.

69. There is an enormous literature on this subject. One of the earliest studies was by Eugène Augeard, *Etude sur la traite des noirs avant 1790 au point de vue du commerce nantais* (Nantes: R. Guist'Hau-A. Dugas, 1901). Many contemporary sources, notably the abbé de Raynal's *Histoire des deux Indes*, remain invaluable to this day. There is a brief and useful summary of the trade in C. L. James, *Black Jacobins, Toussaint L'Ouverture and the San Domingo Revolution* (New York: Randon House, Inc., Vintage Books, 1963).

70. Herbert I. Priestley, *France Overseas through the Old Regime* (New York: Appleton-Century-Crofts, 1939), p. 260.

71. Sombart, *Luxus und Kapitalismus*, pp. 149–50; also Augeard, *Traite des noirs*, pp. 36–37.

72. Taylor, *English Historical Review*, 79 (1964), 487–92.

73. Sombart, *Luxus und Kapitalismus*, p. 9.

74. Marcel Marion, *Histoire financière de la France depuis 1715*, 1, *1715–1789* (Paris: A. Rousseau, 1927), 144.

75. Marion, *Histoire financière*, 1, 152–56.

76. *Mémoires du President Hénault* (Paris: E. Dentu, 1911), pp. 71, 81, 85.
77. Arthur Cobban, *A History of Modern France*, 1, *Old Regime and Revolution* (Baltimore: Penguin Books, Inc., 1957), 57; Marion, *Histoire financière*, p. 203; D. McKie, *Lavoisier* (New York: H. Schuman, 1962), p. 125, originally published 1952.
78. Quoted by Sombart, *Luxus und Kapitalismus*, p. 23.
79. See Taylor, *English Historical Review*, 79 (1964), 489.
80. Taylor, *English Historical Review*, 79 (1964), 492.
81. Sombart, *Der Bourgeois*, p. 46.
82. Sombart, *Luxus und Kapitalismus*, p. 182.
83. Pernoud, *Histoire de la bourgeoisie*, p. 163.
84. Pernoud, *Histoire de la bourgeoisie*, p. 230; Martin, *La grande Industrie en France de 1660 à 1715*, p. 17; Sombart, *Luxus und Kapitalismus*, p. 188; on the historical significance of these concentrations see also Hobsbawm, "Crisis of the seventeenth century."
85. Taylor, *English Historical Review*, 79 (1964), 493–95.
86. See Georges Mathieu, "Notes sur l'industrie en bas-Limousin dans la seconde moitié du XVIII$^e$ siècle," in Julien Hayem, ed., *Mémoires et documents pour servir à l'histoire du commerce et de l'industrie en France*, 1 (Paris: Librairie Hachette S. A., 1911), 35–72; see also *Dictionary of National Biography* sub John Holker.
87. See on this Taylor, *English Historical Review*, 79 (1964), 482–83; Taylor, *American Historical Review*, 72 (1967), 582–83.
88. Taylor, *American Historical Review*, 72 (1967), 487. Similar figures would probably be found for other cities; of 300 bourgeois families in Beauvais, a fair-sized manufacturing city in the seventeenth and eighteenth centuries, Pierre Goubert estimates that about 80 to 100 were families of merchants, the rest being largely *officiers* of various sorts or bourgeois living on their *rentes* [*Familles marchandes sous l'Ancien Régime: les Danse et les Motte, de Beauvais* (Paris: Service d'Edition et de Vente des Productions de l'Education Nationale, 1959), pp. 16–17]. In general, private wealth in France, whether noble or bourgeois, seems to have been overwhelmingly invested in land, buildings, *rentes*, and offices, rather than in enterprises of a capitalist cast in the modern sense. The tendency of the bourgeoisie of the ancien régime to withdraw from commercial activity and transform itself into a landowning, professional, or rentier class has been much commented on and was lamented by contemporaries such as Savary, whose book *Le Parfaict Négociant* appeared at the end of the seventeenth century and expressed the views of mercantilist ministers. (See Sombart, *Der Bourgeois*, pp. 178–80, 361–63 *et passim*; Sagnac, *Formation de la société française*, 2, 175–76, 227–28 *et passim*; Pernoud, *Histoire de la bourgeoisie*, pp. 208–9; also Henri Hauser, "The Characteristic Features of French Economic History from the Middle of the Sixteenth to the Middle of the Eighteenth Century," *Economic History Review*, 4 (1933), 263; Elinor G. Barber, *The Bourgeoisie in Eighteenth-Century France* (Princeton, N. J.: Princeton University Press, 1955), p. 63; Pierre Léon, "L'Industrialisation en France en tant que facteur de croissance économique du début du XVIII$^e$ siècle à nos jours," *Première Conférence Internationale d'Histoire Economique* [Stockholm, 1960] (The Hague: Mouton Publishers, 1960), pp. 163–204, at p. 180.
89. A. Daumard and F. Furet, *Structures et relations sociales à Paris au milieu du XVIII$^e$ siècle* (Paris: Librairie Armand Colin, 1961).
90. Quoted by Kovalewsky, *La France économique*, 2, 60.

91. See Sombart, *Luxus und Kapitalismus*, pp. 152–61, and Hobsbawm, "Crisis of the seventeenth century," pp. 48–51.

92. Sombart, *Luxus und Kapitalismus*, p. 160. Large-scale development of the *grands magasins* did not, of course, occur until the nineteenth century. The oldest of these still in existence—*La Belle Jardinière* and *Les Trois Quartiers*—date from 1824 and 1826 respectively; see Bertrand Gilles, "Sur l'origine des grands magasins parisiens," *Mémoires de la fédération des sociétés historiques et archéologiques de Paris et de l'Ile-de-France*, 7 (1955), 251–64.

93. See Michel Launay, "Madame de Beaugrand et Jean Romilly, horloger, intermédiaires entre Rousseau et Diderot," *Europe*, 41 (1963), 247–63.

94. "Réflexions sur la formation et la distribution des richesses," in *Oeuvres*, ed. G. Schelle, 3, 569–70, quoted by Sée, *L'Evolution commerciale et industrielle de la France sous l'ancien régime* (Paris: M. Giard, 1925).

95. Sée, *Evolution commerciale*, pp. 309–11.

96. Sée, *La France économique et sociale*, p. 106 and Sagnac, *Formation de la société française*, 2, 174–75.

97. Marcel Bouchard, *De l'Humanisme à l'Encyclopédie: essai sur l'évolution des esprits dans la bourgeoisie bourguignonne sous les règnes de Louis XIV et Louis XV* (Paris: Librairie Hachette S. A., 1929).

98. Quoted by F. Delbecke, *L'Action politique et sociale des avocats au XVIIIᵉ siècle* (Louvain: Librairie Universitaire Uystpruyst, 1927; Paris: Editions Sirey, 1927) p. 104. (Translation mine—L. G.)

99. Daumard and Furet, *Structures et relations sociales*, p. 34.

100. Sagnac, *Formation de la société française*, 1, 214–15. Readers of Marivaux will think of Catherine, the old servant of the two Habert sisters in *Le Paysan parvenu*.

101. On rentes, see Taylor, *American Historical Review*, 72 (1967), 480–81 and the article "rentes" in M. Marion, *Dictionnaire des institutions de la France aux XVIIᵉ et XVIIIᵉ siècles* (Paris: Editions A. & J. Picard & Cie. S.A.R.L., 1923) —an invaluable reference work.

102. See "rentes" in Marion's *Dictionnaire*; also his *Histoire financière*, 1, p. 148 *et passim*. On the reduction of rentes after the speculative boom of 1720, see the *Mémoires* of the Paris lawyer Mathieu Marais, 2 (Paris, 1863–68), 58–59.

103. Sombart, *Der Bourgeois*, pp. 195–96.

104. Thus Fontenelle confided to Trublet "qu'il auroit voulu naître avec cinquante mille livres de rente, et d'être Président de la Chambre des Comptes; car . . . il faut être quelque chose, et que ce quelque chose ne vous oblige à rien; que comme son goût le portoit à la composition, il auroit donné souvent à manger, mais sans superfluité ni délicatesse recherchée, à un petit nombre d'amis choisis, jamais plus de cinq ou six à la fois; qu'il leur auroit lu ses ouvrages . . ." [quoted by J. R. Carré, *La philosophie de Fontenelle ou le sourire de la raison* (Paris: Félix Alcan, 1932), p. 506, from Trublet's *Mémoires pour servir à l'histoire de la vie et des ouvrages de M. de Fontenelle* (Amsterdam, 1761), p. 181].

105. Montesquieu, *Esprit des lois*, 23, 15.

106. See Sombart, *Der Bourgeois*, p. 211.

107. See André Burguière, "Société et culture à Reims à la fin du XVIIIᵉ siècle; la diffusion des 'Lumières' analysée à travers les cahiers de doléances," *Annales: Economies, Sociétés, Civilisations*, 1967, pp. 303–39. Burguière shows that the categories in which people expressed their aspirations varied from social group to social group and from trade to trade, the relatively wealthy *miroitiers-*

*tapissiers*, for instance, being more "enlightened," whereas men employed in less-lucrative trades, such as the *tailleurs-fripiers*, remained traditional and relatively conservative.

108. Jaucourt in the *Encyclopédie* distinguishes clearly: "Autrefois, le peuple étoit l'état général de la nation, simplement opposé à celui des grands et des nobles. Il renfermoit les laboureurs, les ouvriers, les artisans, les négocians, les Financiers, les gens de Lettres et les gens de Lois. Mais un homme de beaucoup d'esprit, qui a publié il y a près de vingt ans une dissertation sur la nature du peuple, pense que ce corps de la nation se borne actuellement aux ouvriers et aux Laboureurs" (article "Peuple"). C. B. Macpherson, in a study of seventeenth-century political thought in England, reveals a similar situation there. Even the Levelers, often thought of as the radical democrats of the English revolution, intended to exclude the laboring classes from their proposed franchise, according to Macpherson [*The Political Theory of Possessive Individualism: Hobbes to Locke* (Oxford: Clarendon Press, 1962), pp. 107–36]. Harrington, the author of *Oceana*, treated wage earners and servants—the propertyless —"less as a class within the commonwealth than as a people outside it" (Macpherson, pp. 181–182). Likewise to Locke, "the labouring class was an object of state policy, an object of administration, rather than fully a part of the citizen body" (*ibid.*, p. 224).

109. See Groethuysen, *Welt- und Lebensanschauung*. Babeau, *Artisans d'autrefois*, p. 37, quotes from a book of 1711 called *Le Catéchisme des riches*: "Combien de gens tombent dans la pauvreté parce qu'ils consomment en débauches, en festins et en jeu, le gain qu'ils font par leur travail . . . On voit quelquefois des pauvres qui meurent fort riches; et quoiqu'on ne les approuvent pas à cause qu'ils mendient sans nécessité . . . cependant comme ils sont fort riches parce qu'ils n'ont pas prodigué en folles et vaines dépenses leur gain, il est toujours vrai de dire que les autres auraient pu épargner quelque chose pour subvenir à leurs besoins et imiter ces artisans qui par leur vie réglée trouvent toujours dans leur travail de quoi entretenir leur famille sans être à charge de personne." The significance of the opposition between the "irregular" populace and the "regular," time-conscious bourgeois is brilliantly illuminated in an article by the English historian E. P. Thompson, "Time, Work-Discipline and Industrial Capitalism," *Past and Present*, 38 (1967), 56–97.

110. Quoted by Michel Foucault, *Histoire de la folie à l'âge classique*, ed. 10/18 (Paris: Librairie Plon S.A., 1961), p. 63. See also E. Chill, "Religion and mendicity in seventeenth-century France," *International Review of Social History*, 7 (1962), 400–25; and Pierre Deyon, "A propos du paupérisme au milieu du XVIIᵉ siècle: peinture et charité chrétienne," *Annales: Economies, Sociétés, Civilisations*, 1967, pp. 137–53.

111. Foucault, *Histoire de la folie*, p. 77.

112. Quoted by Pernoud, *Histoire de la bourgeoisie*, 2, 161. As the resources of the state proved inadequate to control mendicity and vagrancy by means of the hôpitaux généraux, however, begging was treated increasingly as a crime punishable by life service at the galleys (Chill, "Religion and mendicity," and Deyon, "A propos du paupérisme").

113. Montesquieu, *Esprit des lois*, 15, 5.

114. Quoted by Pernoud, *Histoire de la bourgeoisie*, 2, 220.

115. *Ibid.*

116. Montesquieu, *Esprit des lois*, 15, 5.

117. Like Fontenelle, moreover, Montesquieu abandoned Descartes's clear distinction

between men and animals, seeing rather a continuous gradation from animal life, through the lower forms of human life, to the higher forms of man; see "Essai sur les causes qui peuvent affecter les esprits et les caractères," *Mélanges inédits* (Bordeaux: G. Gounouilhou, Imprimeur-Editeur; Paris: J. Rouam & Cie., 1892), pp. 129–30. In primitive societies, Montesquieu argues here, nothing activates the mind and men are incapable of adding new ideas to the small store that they have for their basic needs. "On a éprouvé que les sauvages de l'Amérique sont indisciplinés, incorrigibles, incapables de toute lumière et de toute instruction; et en effet, vouloir leur apprendre quelque chose, vouloir plier les fibres de leur cerveau, c'est comme si on entreprenait de faire marcher des gens perclus de tous leurs membres. La grossièreté peut aller à un tel point chez ces nations que les hommes y seront peu différents des bêtes."

118. Taylor, *American Historical Review*, 72 (1967), 487–89.
119. See Mathieu Marais, *Journal et Mémoires*, 3, ed. Lescure (Paris: Firmin-Didot Etude, 1863–68), 188, and Henri de Saint-Simon, *Mémoires*, 37, ed. Boilisle (Paris: Librairie Hachette S.A., 1879–1930), 183–84.
120. See Robert Mandrou, *De la culture populaire aux XVII<sup>e</sup> et XVIII<sup>e</sup> siècles: la Bibliothèque Bleue de Troyes* (Paris: Editions Stock, 1964).
121. Starobinski, *The Invention of Liberty*, trans. Bernard C. Swift (Geneva: Editions d'Art Albert Skira, 1964), p. 74.
122. Babeau, *Artisans d'autrefois*, pp. 58–60.
123. See Sagnac, *Formation de la société française*, 1, 128; Babeau, *Artisans d'autrefois*, pp. 28–31; Edouard Dolléans and Gérard Dehove, *Histoire du travail en France: mouvement ouvrier et législation sociale*, 1, *Des origines à 1919* (Paris: Editions Montchrestien S.A.R.L., 1953), 97–98.
124. See Pernoud, *Histoire de la bourgeoisie*, 2, 162. The holy days were a burden on many countryfolk, on the other hand. One inspector reported to his bishop that "les pauvres se sont plaints que la multitude des Festes augmentait considérablement leur misère." Parish priests had a hard time getting their parishioners to observe the holy days which, together with Sundays, would have required seventy-eight workless days in the year, even after a reform of 1700 eliminating about one-third of the holy days. See Michel Joint-Lambert, "La Pratique religieuse dans le diocèse de Rouen sous Louis XIV, 1660–1715," *Annales de Normandie*, 3 and 4, 1953, 247–74. Other studies of religious practice in the French countryside in the seventeenth and eighteenth centuries bear out these findings; for a general survey of the field, see Gabriel Le Bras, *Etudes de sociologie religieuse* (Paris: Presses Universitaires de France, 1955–1956), especially vol. 1.
125. Sagnac, *Formation de la société française*, 1, 218.
126. Dolléans, *Travail en France*, 1, 100–104; Sée, *La France économique et sociale,* pp. 145–48; Sée, *Evolution commerciale*, pp. 341–46.
127. Hayem, "La répression des grèves au XVIII<sup>e</sup> siècle," *Mémoires et documents*, 1, 93–136.
128. Kovalewsky, *La France économique*, 1, 41.
129. Hayem, *Mémoires et documents*, 1, 93–136.
130. Quoted by Babeau, *Artisans d'autrefois*, p. 35. See also Thompson, *Past and Present*, 38, 56–97.
131. See, for instance, René Passet, *L'Industrie dans la généralité de Bordeaux sous l'intendant Tourny*. Collection de l'Institut d'Economie régionale du Sud-Ouest, 2 (Bordeaux and Paris: Editions Bière, 1954), 139–40.

132. Sée, *La France économique et sociale*, p. 151; Sée, *Evolution commerciale*, pp. 360–63.

133. *Projet d'une dixme royale* (1707), quoted by Kovalewsky, *La France économique*, 1, 388.

134. Sagnac, *Formation de la société française*, 1, 139–43, 218–22.

135. Quoted by Sagnac, *Formation de la société française*, 1, 142.

136. "Réfutation d'Helvétius," *Oeuvres*, 2, ed. Assézat-Tourneux (Paris: Editions Garnier Frères S.A., 1875–77), 428, 429, 431, 440.

137. Letter to Sophie Volland, August 23, 1770, *Correspondance*, 10, ed. G. Roth (Paris: Les Editions de Minuit, 1955–70), 112.

138. "Apologie de l'abbé Galiani," *Oeuvres politiques*, ed. P. Vernière (Paris: Editions Garnier Freres S.A., 1963), p. 84.

139. *Ibid.*, p. 99. Diderot goes on to give an excellent account of the way a unified market gives unlimited scope to the speculator (*ibid.*, pp. 101–3).

140. *Ibid.*, p. 117.

141. *Encyclopédie*, article "Populaire."

142. Quoted by Vernière, *Oeuvres politiques de Diderot*, Introduction, p. xxxiv.

143. *Europe*, January–February, 1963, pp. 78–88.

144. Daniel Mornet, *Origines intellectuelles de la Révolution française, 1715–1787* (Paris: Librairie Armand Colin, 1933), 5th ed. 1954, pp. 420–23.

145. *Essai d'éducation nationale* (1763), quoted by Mornet, *Origines intellectuelles*, p. 423.

Chapter **2**

# SOCIAL CHANGE AND ATTEMPTS AT REFORM IN THE EIGHTEENTH CENTURY

In this chapter we shall consider very summarily some of the changes that occurred in French society in the eighteenth century and the efforts that were made to reform its institutions.

By the end of the seventeenth century Louis XIV's endless military campaigns had put a tremendous strain on almost every sector of French society and the French economy. In the upper ranks of society disaffection was great and growing. The lower orders—the poorer peasants and laborers—were in a virtually permanent, more or less effectively controlled state of unrest, which a bad harvest or a false move on the part of some government official could easily cause to erupt into a riot or a rebellion. It is worth bearing this simple fact in mind when one considers the dissensions in the ranks of the more fortunate classes of society. The truth is that the social conflicts that found ideological expression in the literary and intellectual debates of the eighteenth century occurred *within* the relatively narrow context of a small number of leading social groups whose preeminence rested on the permanent, if tacit repression of the vast majority.

It was thus primarily among the groups whose interests it was the function of the absolutist state to protect and to reconcile that disaffection began to find renewed expression toward the end of the reign of Louis XIV. The private Académie du Luxembourg, which began meeting about 1692, set itself to study the history of government, administration, and institutions in France with a view, ultimately, to reforming the existing

50

order of the state.[1] It was about this time too that Fénelon wrote his historical and political essays, the tendency of which was to restore greater power and influence to the nobility. Criticism of the government came also from the wealthy commercial bourgeoisie of the port towns, which was growing increasingly impatient of Colbert's brand of mercantilism.[2] The older *bourgeoisie de robe,* the higher ranks of which had already penetrated the nobility, was disturbed at its declining influence in relation to other important groups in society, notably the court nobility and the wealthy commercial bourgeoisie. Its opposition was often more sullen than that of the other groups, for it was, more than them, a creation and an instrument of the royal authority—even if the latter was now trying to bypass it by the system of intendants and *lieutenants de police.* But it can be overheard in Boileau's *Satires* and *Epîtres* and in La Bruyère's *Caractères.* It also took the form of reflection on constitutional questions. There were many *robins* as well as great noblemen in the private societies that began meeting in Paris at the end of the seventeenth and in the early decades of the eighteenth century to discuss historical, political, and constitutional questions.

Opposition had thus been mounting during the last decades of Louis XIV's reign, so that when the old king finally died on September 1, 1715 few tears were shed. According to Mathieu Marais and Saint-Simon, the people of Paris rejoiced in the streets. Hundreds of scurrilous epitaphs were circulated.[3]

The hopes of all those who wanted to revive or to extend their power were raised. "Chacun a pensé à ses affaires et à prendre ses avantages dans ce changement," Montesquieu's Usbek wrote to Rhedi.[4] Much was expected from the regency of the duke of Orleans, one of the leaders of the aristocratic opposition to the king in his last days.[5] "On espère beaucoup de sa régence," a provincial in Paris wrote to his correspondent in Burgundy.[6] He had, as Montesquieu remarked, "toutes les qualités d'un bon gentilhomme."[7] For a time, indeed, it looked as though aristocratic government might be restored. In place of the once all-powerful secretaries of state, who were reviled by die-hards such as Saint-Simon as parvenus tyrants bent on destroying the old nobility, the regent set up a system of six councils for war, the navy, finance, home affairs, foreign affairs, and religion—the so-called *Polysynodie*. In so doing he had the support of the parlements as well as of the nobles, since the robe was given an important role in the two councils that interested it most—home affairs and religion —and since the regent had restored to the parlements the right to remonstrate. The Polysynodie experiment was short-lived, however. Four of the councils were abolished in 1722 and the remaining three a year later. Some historians hold that the regent never really intended the system to succeed but regarded it simply as a sop to the aristocratic party.[8] In 1723, according to Sagnac, the monarchy went back to the well-tried form of bureaucratic and centralized government that had been developed under Louis XIV.[9]

But the aristocratic opposition was by no means dead. It survived throughout the century in new combinations and guises. Indeed, the number of factions increased and the play of pressures grew more complex and more difficult to stabilize as the century progressed. Louis XIV had tried to keep court and government apart, respecting the social hierarchy while excluding it from power. The aim of the absolute state was to run the country on behalf of a nobility too divided by faction and intrigue to govern properly. Unfortunately, each new administrative cadre tended to turn into an aristocracy. By the end of the seventeenth century dynasties of intendants were beginning to emerge[10] and in the eighteenth even the fermiers-généraux were transforming themselves into a kind of hereditary aristocracy.[11] As one historian has put it, the absence of effective royal control in the eighteenth century "meant that the machinery of government tended to embed itself in hereditary ruts. Once the king ceased to intervene and to innovate, the institutions that the monarchy had used in order to control the aristocracy became themselves aristocratic."[12] In the course of the eighteenth century the court nobility—estimated at 1 to 5 percent of the total nobility—gained control of the government, so that by 1789 all the ministers were noble with the sole exception of Necker. It also monopolized high positions in the church as well as in the armed forces and the foreign service.

At the same time, the relations of the various social classes to each other were constantly shifting, altering the balance of power within the state. Saint-Simon had refused to cooperate with the parlements and he had disputed their claim to be the representatives of the estates general. In 1721 at the time of the trial of the duc de La Force, however, he and the old guard who still opposed the claims of the parlements found themselves confronting Luxembourg and his allies, who supported them and advocated extending their influence. While the robe and the well-to-do nobility moved closer to one another, the rift between the latter and the poorer provincial nobility deepened, since the main source of income open to the nobility was to be found at court and the purchase of a post at Versailles was beyond the reach of the majority. The court aristocracy with its allies in the robe and the higher circles of finance also found itself in conflict with a rising tide of well-to-do bourgeois. Increasingly, the older nobility tried to preserve for itself as many privileges and offices as possible and to exclude bourgeois and recent anoblis from them. The result was a growing rift between the old nobility on the one hand and the bourgeoisie and anoblis on the other. The bourgeois were doubtless prepared to go along with the ancien régime as long as the passage upward remained open to them, as it had been, one way or another, for centuries. We have seen that they never classed themselves with the *peuple*. But if the doors were to be closed at the very moment when more and more people were eager and able to enter, they might have second thoughts. The slow *embourgeoisement* of the ancien régime might not, after all, be the answer to the needs of the bourgeoisie.

<h1 style="text-align:center">ECONOMIC AND DEMOGRAPHIC
DEVELOPMENTS:
THE CRISIS OF THE 1770s</h1>

All the social tensions and conflicts in the country and in the city were aggravated by the economic and demographic upturn that set in in the second third of the century. This phenomenom is of crucial importance and it should be described briefly. "Les prix montent," writes E. Labrousse, "depuis le début du deuxième tiers du siècle. On sait les conséquences. Ce long mouvement domine tout, met tout en branle. L'esprit d'entreprise est stimulé. La société économique 'tourne' toute seule."[13] The wealthier *fermiers* and the winegrowers, those with surpluses to sell, did well and were encouraged by the steady rise in prices to increase their yield; they invested their money in more land, better buildings, new implements, the clearing of land for cultivation. The seigneurs also benefited. They gradually raised the price of their leases, and made handsome profits on those dues that were paid in kind as a percentage of the farmers' product. Moreover, both they and the bourgeois grain merchants held sufficient stocks to be able to make the most of peak price periods and, when local prices dropped, to export their produce to the highest bidder. Unlike the farmer, the nobleman and the bourgeois did not plow their incomes from the land back into the land. They spent them in the towns where they lived, in consumer goods and in investments in manufactures and trade. Besides, the rural market, on which the most significant sector of industry, textiles, was still dependent, had also expanded. The whole urban economy was thus stimulated by the progress of the rural economy.[14] People spent more on clothing and drank more coffee, they even read the gazette and bought books. And profits in this sector were greater and grew faster than in the rural sector. Moreover, here too profits provided capital to float new enterprises. During the period from 1750 to 1775 the value of industrial production in France doubled, that of trade trebled, and colonial trade increased fivefold. The greatest beneficiaries of the economic upturn were thus the manufacturing and trading bourgeoisie and the part of the aristocracy that had invested its profits in commercial and industrial enterprises.

But all did not do so well out of the economic revival. The mass of

sharecroppers and small farmers had no surplus to sell once they had satis-
fied their own elementary needs, bought their seed for the coming season,
and paid out their taxes and dues in kind. Moreover, the numbers both
of the rural and the urban proletariat were growing apace. A sharp downturn in mortality rates in the second half of the eighteenth century raised
the population of France spectacularly from about 21 million in 1700—
perhaps even fewer in the early decades of the eighteenth century—to
almost 25 million in 1770 and nearly 29 million by 1800.[15] The effect of
this demographic upturn was to ensure a large and cheap labor force for
the expanding economy. For although new developments in industry and
commerce could theoretically absorb large numbers of the new labor force,
this sector was still relatively small. On the other hand, the rural economy
could absorb only limited numbers. All in all, there was an expansion of
the number of employed, and consequently of the total value of earnings,
that is of the market. But whereas the rise in the total value of earnings
was greater than that of prices, the pay of the individual workman was
nowhere near keeping pace with the rise in prices. It rose, but not fast
enough. The position of the urban and rural proletariat had thus worsened
in the age of economic progress and it contrasted starkly with the increasing fortunes of the capitalist and landowning classes and the richer
fermiers.[16]

In the 1770s the economic upswing began to taper off and by 1778
prices were falling all along the line. This development complicated the
broad social opposition of rich and poor, of fermiers, landowners, and
bourgeois on one side and urban and rural workers on the other, which
the period of expansion had produced. The fermiers were hard hit. In the
expansionary period the cost of land leases had *followed* the rise in prices
—and at some distance, since the terms of the lease, which usually lasted
for nine years, were fixed in consideration of prices current at the time of
drawing up the lease. The discrepancy thus benefited the fermier. In a
period of falling prices, of course, the opposite occurred. Prices and
revenue dropped during the period of the lease. But lease rates did not slip.
The demographic upsurge had increased the ranks of the takers and the
farmers could afford to pay. They had not yet dissipated the fortunes
accumulated during the boom period. The great landowners were thus
least hit by the economic crisis. Moreover, they went over to the offen-
sive. What is now known as the "réaction seigneuriale" was a determined
effort on the part of the seigneurs to make up for losses suffered, as a
result of falling prices, on payments made to them in kind, by increasing
the quantity of the latter and reactivating whatever abandoned feudal dues
their lawyers could dig up.

The vast mass of the rural population was even harder hit by the economic decline than the fermiers. Unemployment became widespread and the misery of the rural poor was extreme.

In the towns, some of the luxury trades were sustained for a while by the prosperity of the landowning class but, in general, industry and trade declined. The continued high figures for overseas trade reflect not the prosperity of France as a whole but a sustained volume of trade in colonial produce, which benefited only port cities like Bordeaux and Nantes and of course the plantation owners of Santo Domingo. The all-important textile sector gives a better indication of the state of French trade and industry, and it was lagging badly. The seigneur did well out of the misfortunes of the masses of the rural population, from the well-to-do fermier down to the poorest *journalier*. But in the towns the manufacturing and tradespeople suffered from the decline of business along with their workers, albeit less keenly. The urban workers and a certain section of the bourgeoisie might thus find themselves for a time on the same side of the fence in their resentment of the landowners who alone seemed to be prospering, although they "contributed" nothing—neither labor nor enterprise, nor even much in the way of taxes—to the weal of the state as a whole.

The decline that set in in the 1770s thus had the effect of drawing together, for a time at least, a variety of social groups that were otherwise divided—disgruntled fermiers, poor sharecroppers and day laborers, urban workers (*compagnons* and *maîtres* alike), and bourgeois manufacturers and tradespeople—against the one class that seemed to be doing well out of everybody else's misfortune.

The hostility of those who did not share in the landowners' prosperity was aggravated, moreover, by the inequalities of the fiscal system to which we alluded in the previous chapter. These were the more keenly resented as the boom receded and incomes declined.

It would be incorrect to say that the privileged classes were totally exempt from taxation. The capitation, first introduced in 1695, then abolished, then revived in the eighteenth century, was supposed to affect the entire population. The *vingtième*—originally introduced in 1710 as a *dixième*—was likewise frequently applied in the course of the eighteenth century and was also intended to affect everybody without exception. In fact, the privileged classes wriggled their way out of these taxes. In 1767 Turgot declared that the capitation was applied so disproportionately to the *gentilhomme* and to the *taillable* or peasant that it had become another form of privilege. The same holds good for the vingtième. The tax collectors, intimidated by the noblemen and great robins, failed to carry out their task honestly and effectively. Certain privileged bodies, certain provinces, some corporations were able to settle for a fixed sum, which they agreed to collect among themselves, or even to buy their way out of the tax altogether, for the Treasury could rarely resist the appeal of an assured sum or of an immediate large windfall.[17] Long-term fiscal health was thus frequently sacrificed for a short-term shot in the arm. The parlements, representing the ensemble of the privileged classes, were particularly opposed to the vingtièmes and did everything to obstruct their proper application. In 1789 Du Pont de Nemours wrote that "the Third Estate has observed with utter amazement how the courts (i.e. the parlements) have constantly opposed making the vingtièmes proportionate to income, and how they have made it an unquestionable maxim that there be no verification of the declared value of property and income prior to determining the vingtième, that every ancient abuse in the evaluation of income pass into law and become everlasting, that injustice in the distribution of tax be considered a national privilege."[18]

The peculiar conjuncture of the serious fiscal deficit stemming from the American War, the reduction, as a result of the economic downturn, of revenues from taxes and the impossibility of increasing them to meet the crisis, and the obstinate refusal of the privileged groups to submit to genuine taxation—revealed not only in the attitude of the parlements but in Calonne's failure to persuade the *Assemblée des Notables*, which he convoked in 1787, to come to the aid of the monarchy—proved disastrous to the government. Any one of these factors alone might have been overcome: the combination of them was fatal. Then in 1788 a bad harvest produced a sudden crisis; not the worst of the century perhaps, but sufficient to cause an economy that had only begun to revive a year or so earlier to stumble, then collapse. Textile production, always an important indicator, slumped by 50 percent and other trades showed a similar decline. Unemployment soared, wages began to fall.[19] Discontent was rife in almost all classes of society. The road that led to the Revolution was now clear. Though each social class—the privileged orders, the richer peasants, the bourgeois, the urban workers, and the rural poor—was pulling for itself, all were pulling strongly against the government, which seemed less and less able to cope with the situation. A realignment of the forces of discontent, bringing the people into alliance with the bourgeoisie against the privileged orders, suddenly produced a new political and social crisis, which the ancien régime did not surmount.[20]

The emergence of the bourgeois state, the achievement of the Revolution, had, however, been prepared to some degree in the course of the eighteenth century itself. Not so much, perhaps, through direct action on the part of the bourgeoisie, as indirectly and somewhat paradoxically, through the struggles among the privileged groups and between the privileged groups and the government. In fact, the interests of the bourgeoisie seem to have been less frequently represented directly than carried on the backs, as it were, of one or another of the mutually hostile groups of the ancien régime. Nor is this situation altogether surprising. After all, the bourgeoisie had limited access to the sources of power and decision making. It may not be an accident that the ideal of many *philosophes* was the sage, the spectator, the intellectual who observes from the stalls the comedy being enacted on the stage.[21] The bourgeoisie did not so much think of imposing policies as of seeing certain policies imposed. Indeed, the bourgeois are not found making and breaking ministers or policies—this continued to be largely the work of factions at court—but applauding or criticizing this or that minister, this or that policy. The liberalization of the corn trade was thus desired and campaigned for by powerful aristocratic interests, though in the end freedom of trade, the removal of taxes on industry, the destruction of the guilds, and the substitution of a single tax on ground rent for the cumbersome and inefficient fiscal system of the Old Regime—the stated goals of the Physiocrats—were in fact in the interests of the bourgeoisie too and were, moreover, bound to transform the nation. Similarly, it was the government through its successive comptrollers general that—as the parlements charged—began to whittle away the privileges of the first two "orders," and yet it did so obviously without revolutionary intent but in response to the needs of the existing social order.

Let us look briefly at two areas—economic policy and fiscal policy —in which, as we have suggested, the Old Regime itself initiated changes that tended to alter its very nature and to begin its transformation into a bourgeois state.

## ATTEMPTS AT ECONOMIC REFORM

One of the most notable consequences of the boom from the 1740s to the 1770s was the progressive withdrawal of the state from the economic sphere and the collapse or at least the weakening of established political and economic institutions and values. "Dès lors que l'économie va toute seule," writes Labrousse, "l'Etat tend à s'abstenir. Il s'en remet à l'entrepreneur, il abdique entre ses mains. L'interventionnisme recule."[22] Egged on by the prospering landowners, reassured by the theoretical writings of the Physiocrats or *économistes*, which provided a satisfying "philosophical" rationale for the removal of trade restrictions, the enlightened ministers of the last half century of the ancien régime made repeated attempts to lift longstanding regulations hampering the free internal and international movement of grain. While the philosophes and the économistes participated in a heated debate on the subject—Voltaire, Diderot, and Galiani entered the fray, to mention only three—the ministers confronted political and economic realities. They had to contend with serious disorders sparked off by bad harvests and rising bread prices, disorders that were exploited and perhaps even fomented by political factions at court.[23] It was by no means plain sailing all the way for the freetraders. There were setbacks especially between 1766 and 1769, culminating in the rescinding by Terray in 1770 of the liberalization measures adopted by Bertin and L'Averdy in 1763 and 1764. Nor was Turgot's reactivation of the 1763 edict in 1774 the end of the story. But the fight was on, led by certain of the king's ministers and supported by the wealthy landowners, for the freeing of the corn trade and the end of state intervention in economic matters.

The same spirit of economic liberalism decided the fate of another old established economic institution in the second half of the eighteenth century—the guilds or corporations. Under Colbert and well into the first half of the eighteenth century, the state had, on the whole, favored the guilds, but during the boom period it began to withdraw its support.[24] In 1750 Machaut, the comptroller general, instructed the intendants to make an inquiry into the operations of the guilds. Gournay at Lyons in 1752 and Le Bret, intendant of Brittany, in 1755, drew up reports criticizing their exclusiveness. In 1761 Bertin proposed that guild regulations be simplified and liberalized. Fifteen years later Turgot decreed, in the name of the "natural right to work," that all men were free thenceforth to exercise whatever craft they wanted to or were able to. All associations of masters and of workers alike were forbidden. Though Turgot's edict had to be modified very considerably a few months later, the process of "reform" went on; from 1776 to the Revolution various efforts were made to simplify the statutes of the guilds and to eliminate obstacles to new techniques or to a larger recruitment of workers. In the end, the Constituent Assembly reactivated the reforms that Turgot had failed to carry through.

The process of economic "liberalization"—that is, of withdrawal of the state from the economic sphere—that was fulfilled after the Revolution was thus in fact actively initiated by the ancien régime itself in its last half century. Labrousse sums up this development in the concluding pages of the introduction to his important book *La Crise de l'économie française à la fin de l'ancien régime et au début de la Révolution:*

> Since the economy is running by itself, the State tends to stand back. It hands over the reins to the entrepreneur and abdicates its functions to him. Interventionism ceases to be government policy. . . . Thus the royal power dismembered itself. Thus the Economy and the State were separated. Thus the class of heads of enterprises—made up indifferently of nobles, bourgeois and peasants, but dominated by the bourgeoisie—

advanced in wealth and independence. . . . Success no longer depended on the State. . . . Better still. The economic abdication of the monarchy was complemented by its social abdication. The monarchy handed over to the entrepreneur not only the responsibility for making the machine run but the responsibility for providing a livelihood for the fastest growing sector of the population. The *Conseil* showed increasing hostility to salary rates approved by municipal authorities: the entrepreneur had to be given a free hand. Above all, it is not the function of the law to ensure a means of subsistence in kind to the starving masses of the countryside by maintaining a certain acreage of common lands and upholding old common claims on the land of the rich; the entrepreneurs themselves, rural and urban, must ensure that the masses find the means of subsistence through the hire of their labor. The policy of confidence in profit, encouraged by a long period of capitalist prosperity, thus had a twofold effect: at the same time as it freed the bourgeoisie from control by the State, it placed a large part of the nation in its power.[25]

## ATTEMPTS AT FISCAL REFORM

Fiscal reform too was initiated by the ministers of the ancien régime themselves in their efforts to keep the state, as constituted, financially solvent. Without attacking the basic fiscal structure, Noailles, Orry, Bertin, L'Averdy, and others, with the support of many of the intendants, tried to reform the taille so that it would at least be properly distributed among those who were subject to it.[26] In some provinces attempts were made to reform the corvées by commuting them into a monetary obligation and spreading the load more evenly. These modest efforts at reform encountered fierce resistance, however, not so much from the peasantry, whose suspicions could be allayed, as from the privileged groups and their champions, the parlements. The fiscal history of the eighteenth century is in fact largely that of an unrelenting struggle between the privileged orders and their government, with the latter trying to introduce some changes in order to shore up the status quo and the former absolutely refusing to cooperate.

The earliest inroads upon the fiscal immunities of the privileged orders took the form of extraordinary impositions in time of war, such as the capitation of 1695. They were not very rigorously applied. All kinds of exceptions and accommodations were made.[27] The dixième of 1710 was a more important measure, but once more the clergy and various corporate bodies, provinces, towns, and so on bought themselves out for a fraction of what they ought to have contributed; once more the wealthy and privileged used their influence to intimidate the collectors; once more there was no proper basis for assessment and no uniformity in the collection of the tax. In 1733 and in 1741 when the dixième was reintroduced the same thing happened again. "Le clergé persiste à ne verser que des dons gratuits. La noblesse ne fait point de déclaration, ou ne les fait que dérisoires, ne paye pas, brave les saisies, sûre qu'on n'osera pas en venir à cette extrémité, et fait en définitive reculer préposés, huissiers, sergents, et intendant."[28] Influential persons were always able to have their already low assessments reduced still further until they became a joke. They were aided and abetted by the parlements, the *Cour des Aides* and other similar bodies, which lost no opportunity of obstructing the work of the government and its agents, as successive ministers were to discover. Under the Regency, John Law's proposal for fiscal, administrative, and judicial reforms, which would have strengthened the hand of the central government, won him the undying hatred of the parlements and the nobility.[29] Montesquieu spoke for all of them when he complained that "il voulait ôter les rangs intermédiaires et anéantir les corps politiques." Likewise under the duc de Bourbon, Pâris Duverney and the comptroller Dodun were bitterly opposed by the parlements for their efforts to reduce privilege and to end abuses in the administration, such as the use of Treasury funds by the agents of the fisc for their own purposes. Above all the privileged classes were outraged by Duverney's *cinquantième*. This tax was to apply to all without exception; it was introduced in time of peace, implying therefore that the privileged orders were *ordinarily* subject to taxation; and it was to be an *impôt en nature,* which meant that, although it might be difficult to administer, it would not be possible to get around it as easily as the dixième of 1710. The parlements raised a storm of protest, and the edict establishing it had to be registered in a *lit de justice.* Provincial governments refused to register it. The clergy appealed to the pope and reaffirmed the immunity from taxation of all ecclesiastical wealth.[30] As always, it was easy for the privileged to exploit the resentments and difficulties of the peasants, who were hard hit by a bad harvest and a severe shortage of food. All available means were used to harass the tax assessors and to prevent the peasants from making their declarations. The government could hardly find the men to apply the tax or the information to prepare adequately reliable lists. Yet Duverney held firm. On the eve of the harvest of 1726, however, he was brought down in the wake of Bourbon and Madame de Prie. This ministerial revolution was so apropos, in Marion's view, that it is reasonable to guess it was engineered by the groups opposed to the tax. The ministry of Fleury, which followed, was prudent, hostile to change, "rassurante pour les privilégiés, surtout pour le clergé."[31] The new comptroller general, Le Pelletier Desforts, decreed that the cinquantième would not be levied in kind, that those privileged bodies that had bought themselves out before could do so again, and that the tax would be collected in accordance with the old tax rolls of 1710.

Fleury sought stability in the finances by submitting to established practices and malpractices and alienating as few powerful people as possible while keeping out of wars and avoiding unnecessary expenditure. Likewise Orry, who succeeded Desforts as comptroller general in 1730, tried to effect economies at court. The War of the Polish Succession required a reactivation of the dixième in 1733 and again in 1741 but, as we saw, these taxes were applied in such a way as to give little offense to the privileged. In 1745 Orry was replaced by Machault d'Arnouville, intendant of Valenciennes, whose task was to raise funds to finance the War of the Austrian Succession. As soon as the Peace of Aix-la-Chapelle had been signed, however, Machault set himself to the task of general fiscal reform. The king had promised that the dixième would be withdrawn as soon as the war ended. Machault therefore introduced a new vingtième in which he—and his enemies—saw the basis of far-reaching fiscal reform. No privileged body (provinces or clergy), he decreed, was to be allowed to buy itself out. Above all, the fact that the new vingtième was introduced in time of peace, not to meet an extraordinary expense but to provide for the running-down of the debt, and with no stipulation as to when it would be withdrawn, marked a notable departure from previous practice. Moreover, Machault instructed his tax collectors to draw up an accurate *cadastre* or roll of taxable wealth—the great goal of all the fiscal reformers of the ancien régime.

In fact, his men were not equal to the task. There were not enough of them, some of them were lazy or ignorant, and few were not subject at one point or another to persuasion or intimidation by the wealthy and influential. Still, even this imperfect bureaucracy might have carried through some reforms. Realizing this, the nobility, the estates, the clergy, and the parlements threw themselves into the fight against Machault. In the end they brought him down with the help of the *dévot* party at court.[32] The support of Voltaire and the philosophes[33] was doubtless gratifying to him, but practically useless.

The Seven Years' War (1756–1763) put new strains on the finances. Borrowings, anticipations of revenue, the mortgaging of reserves were resorted to on a larger scale than ever. Again a comptroller general tried to institute reforms. At the end of 1763 Bertin, hoping to touch the pockets of the privileged classes, prolonged the vingtième into peacetime for a period of six years and gave instructions that it should be levied on the basis of an up-to-date and accurate assessment of all wealth, with no exceptions. Again the parlement, encouraged by previous successors, and conscious of the backing of all the privileged classes, refused to cooperate. At Grenoble and Toulouse writs were issued against the governors, who were to have the edicts registered in these cities, and they had to protect themselves with an armed guard from the bailiffs of the courts. There were similar disturbances elsewhere.[34] Once more the comptroller had to climb down. The parlements got the government to concede that the ving-tièmes could be levied on the basis of the existing tax rolls. At a time of rising land values and revenues this was a notable victory.

The intractability of the parlements was bound to lead to another showdown. It came in 1771, the occasion being provided by a dispute between the commandant of Brittany, d'Aiguillon, and La Chalotais, attorney general in the parlement of Rennes. By a series of provocations Maupeou, the keeper of the seals, enticed the parlements into open defiance of the king's authority on this issue and then in January of 1771, by *lettres de cachet,* he exiled the magistrates, not as had happened before, to pleasant country towns not too far from Paris, but to the remote mountain villages of Auvergne. The venal offices of the parlementaires were abolished without compensation, and new courts were instituted, in which justice was to be free. At the same time, far-reaching judicial reforms were planned, which were later carried through by Maupeou's secretary, Lebrun, when he became third consul during the Consulate of Bonaparte.

Maupeou's *coup d'état* gave Terray, the comptroller general, a free hand with the finances. In 1771 he made the vingtième virtually permanent, set up new schools for training tax collectors, and instructed the intendants to have their tax controllers make the necessary investigations for drawing up the new tax rolls. As always, it was this inspection of their affairs that the privileged groups could not tolerate. The parlements had been disarmed but the intendants, who were responsible for maintaining order in their intendancies, either did not themselves wish to see the reforms put through or judged them inopportune in view of the bad feeling caused by the destruction of the parlements.

It is characteristic of governmental efforts at fiscal reform that Maupeou and Terray were widely unpopular. They had attacked the privileged groups but they had also alienated the financiers and the *rentiers* and their highhanded autocratic methods lost them the support of the bourgeoisie. Only Voltaire took up their cause. Diderot disliked them[35] and Beaumarchais's widely read *Mémoires* against Goezman, a Maupeou judge, helped to mobilize opinion against them. With no support other than that of the king and a small faction at court, Maupeou and Terray were ousted on the death of Louis XV and the accession of the new monarch, and all their work was undone. The parlements were allowed to return, to the great jubilation of all the privileged groups. At Rennes, La Chalotais was escorted into the city by 200 gentlemen on horseback, and a long line of aristocratic carriages brought up the rear of the procession. The new comptroller general, Turgot, who had supported the return of the parlements, even though he had no illusions about them, quickly ran into the same difficulties as all his predecessors.

Turgot had moved in circles close to the philosophes, and his advent was enthusiastically hailed by the bourgeoisie. He had, indeed, many plans for fiscal reform. He would probably, had he remained in office long enough, have abolished the taille and vingtième and replaced them both with a straightforward and equitably assessed tax on all landowners, irrespective of their class.[36] He did in fact eliminate some abuses from the operations of the *ferme générale* and it was widely rumored that he planned to abolish the ferme altogether. These stories did not increase his popularity among the financiers and the entrenched privileged groups. Nevertheless, Turgot understood that the speed at which he could move was determined by the administrative cadres at his disposal and that it was useless to institute reforms before every detail had been meticulously planned and the means of application made available. The reforms he actually sought to bring about were therefore fairly modest.

Two measures introduced in 1776 were far-reaching enough, however, to unleash violent opposition. One was the abolition of the guilds, already referred to, the other was the abolition of the corvées and their replacement by a tax to be levied on all landowners, no matter what their status, in proportion to their incomes. Even within the ministry Turgot by no means enjoyed the unanimous support of his colleagues for these measures. Indeed, Miromesnil, the keeper of the seals, was actively opposed to them and sympathized with Turgot's enemies in the parlements and at court.

The dialogue constituted by Miromesnil's comments on the edict of 1776 and Turgot's reply not only reveals clearly what was at stake but raises the whole question of fiscal reform to a level of discussion at which the political implications of reform are spelled out and the antagonism of the two sides is made thoroughly clear. After some criticisms of detail that Turgot easily rebutted, Miromesnil affirmed that the privileged classes were already the most heavily burdened and that they had no real advantage over the taillables.[37] Turgot seized on this fantastic claim and proceeded to enumerate, point by point, the substantial advantages enjoyed by the privileged.[38] Miromesnil's principal argument was not factual, however, but political and constitutional. With its echoes of Montesquieu, it was typical of aristocratic complaints and parliamentary remonstrances. "Il est difficile de changer tout à coup le génie, le caractère, les préjugés mêmes d'une grande nation," he warned, "il n'est peut-être pas sage de le tenter."[39] The privileges of many offices, purchased by the well-to-do, need not be defended (so much for those bourgeois who had recently bought their way into the privileged classes; they could be sacrificed without question!), but those of the nobility guaranteed that ardent sense of honor which was the very foundation of the monarchy. It is in the king's own interests to respect the privileges of the first two orders, since the division of France into three great orders, each with its rights, its privileges, "peut-être ses préjugés," is the very foundation and support of the monarchy.[40]

Turgot answered that whatever the historical reasons for the privileges of the nobility and the clergy, they were not easy to justify in the second half of the eighteenth century. The nobles no longer did military service in return for land. If they served in the army, they were paid for their trouble. Indeed the army had become a profession, and it was itself a large item in the king's finances, burdened as it was by far too many lucrative offices that were the preserve of the nobility and of which the holders were often woefully inept. Above all, there was no justification for the idea that the nobility should be exempt from taxation. Turgot was careful to point out that he had no intention of destroying all the privileges of the nobility. He had read his Montesquieu too and he knew "aussi bien que tout autre qu'il ne faut pas toujours faire le mieux qu'il est possible."[41] The statesman had a duty to correct "les défauts d'une constitution ancienne" but he must do so slowly as events and public opinion permit. So there was no question of extending the taille to the nobility and clergy. In practice, therefore, Turgot intended to introduce his reforms prudently, but in theory he was ready for the abolition of privileges. And his argument reveals how much this royal administrator, whose primary aim was to restore the finances and the economy of the Old Regime, was influenced by modes of thought that were, as Miromesnil held, foreign to the traditional social order of the Old Regime.

In the end the privileged classes succeeded, as they had succeeded on every previous occasion, in bringing down the minister who threatened their interests. On May 12, 1776, Louis XVI dismissed the last great reforming minister of the ancien régime and in the course of the summer all his work was systematically undone.

In the years that followed the regime struggled along mostly on the strength of loans. Indeed it became one of the requirements of a good finance minister that he should be able, somehow or other, to maintain credit and float even more new loans in the face of leaping deficits. No one cared to hear either of the seriousness of the financial situation or of reforms. The administration of the finances in the Old Regime, its bookkeeping, was in any case so complicated that it was not easy to find out exactly what the situation was. On the other hand, it was possible to disguise it and make it seem better than it was. To their skill in doing this and in finding expedients that made reforms seem unnecessary Necker (1776–1781) and Calonne (1783–1787) owed their prodigious popularity, though the latter did not keep his when he ultimately revealed the truth to the *Assemblée des Notables* in 1787 and outlined a program of reforms. "Il s'agit aujourd'hui d'anéantir  .  .  .  les abus des privilèges pécuniaires, les exceptions à la loi commune, et tant d'exemptions injustes qui ne peuvent affranchir une partie des contribuables qu'en aggravant le sort des autres," he declared.[42] Provincial assemblies were to be set up, similar to those Turgot had had in mind, that is to say, composed of landowners with at least 600 livres income and without any other distinction of rank, to help with the implementation of new taxes.

The privileged orders got the point. "Savez-vous que cette mauvaise plaisanterie (the assemblées provinciales) me coûtera au moins 300,000 livres de rente," the duke of Orleans remarked to the marquis de Bouillé. "Comment cela, monseigneur?" "Avec les intendants, je m'arrange, je paie à peu près ce que je veux; les administrations provinciales, au contraire, me feront payer à la rigueur."[43] It was almost inevitable, in view of the stand he had taken, that Calonne would be overthrown, and he was, in April 1787, not on account of his earlier prodigalities but on account of his proposed remedies. As Chamfort said, he was left alone while he set the house on fire and he was chased out when he sounded the alarm. By refusing to believe Calonne—or affecting not to believe him—and by ignoring his appeal to them to cooperate in effecting the reforms that alone might have saved the Old Regime, the privileged classes revealed not only their own irresponsibility, but the insoluble divisions within the Old Regime. The only remedy for its ills, the remedy that successive comptrollers general had all proposed sooner or later, would indeed so radically have altered the complexion of the patient that it is not surprising the privileged orders refused it. In the end, however, other powerful elements in the society—and these included not only the well-to-do bourgeoisie but aristocrats who were confident that they stood to profit more from a free market than from old privileges—carried through the necessary reforms with the help of the discontented masses.

## NOTES

1. E. Carcassonne, *Montesquieu et le problème de la constitution française* (Paris: Presses Universitaires de France, 1926), pp. 7–8.
2. Lionel Rothkrug, *Opposition to Louis XIV: the political and social origins of the French Enlightenment* (Princeton, N. J.: Princeton University Press, 1965), and Philippe Sagnac, *La Formation de la société française moderne*, 1, *La société et la monarchie absolue, 1661–1715* (Paris: Presses Universitaires de France, 1945), 160–62.
3. Mathieu Marais, *Journal et Mémoires*, 1, ed. Lescure (Paris: Firmin-Didot Etude, 1863–68), 192; Henri de Saint-Simon, *Mémoires*, 28, ed. Boilisle (Paris: Librairie Hachette, S.A., 1879–1930), 377–78; Emile Raunié, ed., *Chansonnier historique du XVIIIᵉ siècle*, 1 (Paris: A. Quantin, 1879), 1–68.
4. *Lettres persanes*, letter 92; also Saint-Simon, *Mémoires*, 28, 375–76, on the court: "Les uns, en espérance de figurer, de se mêler, de s'introduire étoient ravis de voir finir un règne sous lequel il n'y avoit rien pour eux à attendre; les autres, fatigués d'un joug pesant, toujours accablant . . . étoient charmés de se trouver

au large; tous, en général, d'être délivrés d'une gêne continuelle, et amoureux des nouveautés."

5. See Montesquieu's comments in praise of him in "Lettres de Xénocrate à Phérès" (1723), "Eloge historique du maréchal de Berwick" and "Pensées," *Oeuvres complètes*, ed. Daniel Oster (Paris: Editions du Seuil, 1964), pp. 154–56, 841, 1024.

6. Bibliothèque Nationale, Mss. Bréquigny, 66, fol. 69.

7. "Pensées," *Oeuvres complètes*, p. 937.

8. Sagnac, *Formation de la société française*, 2, 1–5; cf. the contemporary views of Saint-Simon, *Mémoires*, 29, 53.

9. Sagnac, *Formation de la société française*, 2, 5.

10. A. D. Lublinskaya, *Vnutrennaya Politika Frantsuskovo Absolutisma, 1633–1649* (Moscow and Leningrad: Izdatel'stvo "Nauka," 1966), quoted by J. H. M. Salmon, "Venality of office and popular sedition in seventeenth-century France," *Past and Present*, 37 (1967), 21–43.

11. See Norman Hampson, *A Social History of the French Revolution* (London: Routledge & Kegan Paul Ltd., 1963), p. 16. In 1780 the succession of the *fermiers généraux* was restricted to the sons of *fermiers*, which made the group virtually a closed caste.

12. Hampson, *History of the French Revolution*, pp. 2–3.

13. C. E. Labrousse, *La Crise de l'économie française à la fin de l'ancien régime et au début de la Révolution* (Paris: Presses Universitaires de France, 1943), p. xxiii.

14. I have followed Labrousse, but on this point especially his thesis has been questioned, notably by David S. Landes, *Journal of Economic History*, 10 (1950), 195–211.

15. Louis Henry in D. V. Glass and D. E. C. Eversley, *Population in History: Essays in Historical Demography* (London: E. J. Arnold & Son Ltd., 1965), pp. 434–56.

16. Labrousse, *Crise de l'économie française*, pp. xxxi–xxxii.

17. See Marcel Marion, *Machault d'Arnouville* (Paris: Librairie Hachette S. A., 1891), p. 20 and the same author's *Dictionnaire des institutions de la France aux XVIIe et XVIIIe siècles* (Paris: Editions A. & J. Picard & Cie. S.A.R.L., 1923), article "Capitation."

18. Marion, *Dictionnaire des institutions*, article "Vingtième." (Translation mine—L. G.)

19. Labrousse, *Crise de l'économie française*, pp. xl–xli.

20. For a brief account of the way the collaboration of *peuple* and bourgeoisie was crystallized on the eve of the Revolution see George Rudé, "The Outbreak of the French Revolution," *Past and Present*, 8 (1955), 28–42.

21. *Cf.*, for instance, Diderot, "Paradoxe sur le comédien": "Dans la grande comédie, la comédie du monde, celle à laquelle je reviens toujours, toutes les âmes chaudes occupent le théâtre; tous les hommes de génie sont au parterre" [*Oeuvres*, ed. Assézat-Tourneux, 8 (Paris: Editions Garnier Freres S. A., 1875–77), 368].

22. Labrousse, *Crise de l'économie française*, p. xlix.

23. Douglas Dakin, *Turgot and the Ancien Régime in France* (London: Methuen & Co., Ltd., 1939), pp. 180–94.

24. There is, however, some evidence of government opposition to restrictive guild practices before the 1730's; see A. Hertzberg, *The French Enlightenment and the Jews* (New York: Columbia University Press, 1968), chap. 4–5.

25. Labrousse, *La Crise de l'économie française*, pp. xlix–l.

26. See Marcel Marion, *L'Impôt sur le revenu au XVIIIe siècle* (Toulouse: Edouard

Privat & Cie. S. A., 1901), pp. 36–69 (Bibliothèque méridionale, 2nd series, vol. 7).

27. Marion, *Machault d'Arnouville*, pp. 20–21.
28. *Ibid.*, p. 23.
29. Marcel Marion, *Histoire financière de la France depuis 1715*, 1 (Paris: A. Rousseau, 1927), 90–107.
30. *Ibid.*, pp. 131–32; also Ernest Lavisse, *Histoire de France*, Vol. 8, Part 2 (Paris: Librairie Hachette S. A., 1900–11), 81–82.
31. Marion, *Histoire financière*, 1, p. 134.
32. Lavisse, *Histoire de France*, Vol. 8, Part 2, 236–37.
33. See *Voltaire's Correspondence*, ed. T. Besterman, §3394 (Les Délices: Institut et Musée Voltaire, 1953–65), and the satirical "Extrait du décret de la Sacrée Congrégation de l'Inquisition de Rome à l'encontre d'un libelle intitulé *Lettres sur le vingtième*," *Oeuvres*, ed. Moland, 23 (Paris: Editions Garnier Freres S. A., 1877–85), 463–64; also *Siècle de Louis XV*, chap. 26.
34. Lavisse, *Histoire de France*, Vol. 8, Part 2, 366–67 and Marion, *Impôt sur le revenu*, pp. 188–90.
35. See "Réfutation d'Helvétius," *Oeuvres*, 2, ed. Assézat-Tourneux, 380, and "Neveu de Rameau," *ibid.*, 5, 395.
36. Dakin, *Turgot and the Ancien Régime*, pp. 168–70.
37. *Oeuvres de Turgot*, 5, ed. G. Schelle (Paris: Félix Alcan, 1913–23), 168–69.
38. *Ibid.*, pp. 170–73.
39. *Ibid.*, p. 189.
40. *Ibid.*, pp. 182, 193.
41. *Ibid.*, p. 184.
42. Quoted by Marion, *Histoire financière*, 1, 388.
43. Quoted *ibid.*, p. 389.

# Chapter **3**

# **ENLIGHTENMENT**

It is generally agreed today that the conditions and traditions of expression in each of the fields of cultural activity determine to a considerable extent what is done within those fields. Literature, painting, philosophy impose their own laws on those who practice them, and it can even be argued that each of these cultural series has a time or history of its own, independent of chronological time. The notion of a homogeneous time of history, in short, is open to question. It seems unlikely, however, that different forms of human activity at any given time are wholly unrelated,[1] that there is no connection between, say, the breakdown of the feudal social order in western Europe and a shift of the center of philosophical inquiry from the whole created world, of which man is a part, to the nature of man himself, the observer of a world over against which he stands apparently alone. Nonetheless, no total system of explanation commands widespread adherence today. The Marxist approach to cultural phenomena, in particular, has come under constant fire on the grounds that it does not take sufficient account of the specificity of cultural activities. It is also objected that really significant cultural patterns and changes concern not so much the content of thought as categories and systems of classification.

While recognizing that many methodological problems remain unresolved and that my interpretations are in no way complete, I shall attempt in the following pages to suggest some of the ways in which the sets of ideas, or rather the ways of looking at the world, to which we normally refer by the term "Enlightenment," can be considered responses to a concrete historical situation—means by which men took cognizance of their situation, formulated their problems, and to some degree attempted to resolve those problems.

As we investigate these ideas, however, we should bear in mind that a very large section of the population was never able to organize its attitudes, values, and aspirations in this way at all, having neither the leisure nor the training to do so. It expressed itself as best it could in the only framework available to it, that of religious practices and beliefs, or in explosions of violence, short-lived revolts that the established order with its superior organization was usually able to put down. The outbursts of religious fervor—"enthusiasm" as the better off and better organized said contemptuously—that sometimes accompanied these revolts and gave a loose form to the feelings of the masses, were usually as poorly organized and had consequently as little staying power as the revolts themselves. The Camisards in the south of France at the end of the seventeenth and the beginning of the eighteenth century and the Convulsionnaires and their millenarian successors in the poorer quarters of Paris in the thirties and forties of the eighteenth century provide two examples of such outbursts. The history of ideas in the Enlightenment is thus in large measure the history of the ideas that circulated in the upper classes of society.

## THE FRENCH TRADITION: CARTESIAN OPTIMISM

It is widely held—and not only by Marxists—that the Enlightenment elaborated an ideology for the modern bourgeoisie and for the modern bourgeois democratic state. Yet it is strange that it was in France, where capitalism and industrialism had made very modest inroads and where leading elements in the bourgeoisie had come to form a kind of aristocracy, that the most radical theoretical formulations of the Enlightenment were produced, rather than in England where capitalism was far more deeply entrenched.[2] This is surely an important historical problem, particularly if a relation is supposed between the history of ideas and social history.[3] We shall begin by addressing ourselves to it, in the hope not so much of finding answers as of stimulating discussion.

If we accept, even with reservations, that the extension and intensification of capitalist economic relations in the countries of western Europe was accompanied by a transformation of the superstructure of society—that is to say not only the legal and institutional relations among men in society but the expression of men's experience of their relations to each other in works of philosophy, political theory, art, literature, even science —it will be useful to distinguish the phases that mark this transformation.

Franz Borkenau considers three such phases: the penetration into the mass of the population of an ethics favorable to capitalism, the creation of a new theoretical view of the world, and the creation of a political and legal order appropriate to capitalism.[4] These three developments occurred unevenly according to Borkenau; in addition, the order in which they occurred was not the same in the main Western European countries. Highly industrialized as it was, England depended for a long time on semi-feudal legal forms; conversely in France, the introduction of a coherent legal system appropriate to capitalist society after the Revolution did not prevent many traditional and precapitalist attitudes and ways of life from continuing well into the nineteenth century. The order in which the three developments took place, moreover, affected the concrete form that capitalist society took in any given country.

The earliest and most thoroughly capitalist countries were perhaps those in which the spread of capitalism was anticipated by the spread of an ethics favorable to its development. In those countries the new mass ethics—provided by Calvinism or Puritanism—did not follow logically, as it were, from the economic situation itself; on the contrary, it seems to have found its champions in social groups that were adversely affected by the breakdown of feudal relations, the growth of a money economy, the spread of cottage industry, and the increasing power of merchant-entrepreneurs.[5] The new ethics was one not of withdrawal from the world but of struggle within it. It was thus different from the neo-Stoicism that was fairly widespread in educated and aristocratic circles in the late sixteenth and seventeenth centuries. Not that the account of man's situation in the contemporary world provided by neo-Stoicism was in all respects at variance with that of Calvinism. Certain views were common to both: the individual is alienated from society; social processes are impenetrable; there is nothing stable in the world; the only significant motive for human activity is desire and greed; the right should be pursued, but men should not set their happiness by it, since in a disordered and irrational world the outcome of one's actions is unforeseeable. But neo-Stoicism was shot through with elitism. It was the philosophy of a well-to-do class that sought to adapt its modes of thought and feeling to a new social reality, not with a view to active life in the world, but rather with a view to withdrawal from the world. Since they could not alter the world, the "wise" would alter their attitude to it. Neo-Stoicism was thus an ethics of withdrawal and contemplation for the relatively comfortable few; the new ethics that proved so favorable to capitalist development, according to Troeltsch, Weber, and others, was, on the other hand, as one would expect, an ethics of participation and action for all. Not surprisingly, since it attempted to justify a life of hard work and uncertain success, it assumed an irrational, religious form. In the sixteenth and seventeenth centuries unremitting labor did not yet seem either a natural or normal form of behavior for everyone, as it came to do later in the heyday of industrial capitalism. Only within the framework of an irrational religion could it be made to appear normal. One can understand that two doctrines which lay at the heart of Calvinism might have held particular appeal for the hard-pressed smaller gentry and artisans of the sixteenth and seventeenth centuries: the radical evil of natural man and the natural world, forsaken by God, and the irrational commands of a God, who, by human criteria, would be regarded as cruel and unjust. For the Calvinist God demands unrelenting moral effort, although this effort cannot be rationally justified, since it has no relation to salvation, to success, or to personal happiness.

It may be that in England the very success of the irrational ideology which supported capitalism rendered any far-reaching attempts to face and resolve theoretically the problems and contradictions of capitalist society to some degree unnecessary. Once the medieval Catholic idea of a divinely instituted and sanctioned order of nature and society was abandoned in consequence of the extreme emphasis on original sin and the corruption of nature, on the *distance* between man and God, the study of nature and of man in the world could be released from the framework of a total philosophy and given over to practical, empirical investigation. Various domains of study were thus at the same time "detheologized" and fragmented; they were no longer controlled by a total philosophy; nor, however, did they constitute one. The ideal of a total rational world view in which everything was interconnected with everything else was abandoned in favor of a world view that allowed for empirically based systematizations of separate areas.[6]

After the collapse of Calvinism, Jansenism was the only religious ideology that might perhaps have achieved in France the kind of ethical and intellectual revolution which Puritanism achieved in England. In fact, however, Jansenism was never as thoroughly irrational as Calvinism. The Jansenists never adopted the doctrine of salvation by faith alone and they insisted upon the constant struggle within man between rationality and irrationality, good and evil, our "true" nature and our "fallen" nature. Jansenism required in practice a profound effort at sanctification. Strict obedience to God's positive commands was not enough. The Jansenist was required to seek an insight into the organizing principle of all moral behavior, the love of God; particular acts acquired a positive moral character if they were done for love of God, not if they were done in mere fearful obedience to the commands of a tyrant.

Jansenism thus made demands that only a small circle of saints could fulfill and in fact it never did become a popular religious movement, except in certain areas and in a somewhat special form. Its influence on the conduct of everyday life was immeasurably slighter than that of Calvinism.

Moreover, it never developed anything like the Puritan doctrine of vocation. For one thing, Jansenism, like orthodox Catholicism, did not include the belief that everyone had a vocation in the world—indeed it was extremely sympathetic to the contemplative monastic orders—and its conception of vocation was closer to the Lutheran one of passive submission to God's will than to the Calvinist one of ceaseless activity to increase God's glory. On the whole, therefore, Jansenism was both incompatible with the day-to-day pursuits of the most active bourgeois and unfavorable to strenuous efforts in this world. Indeed it was, if anything, more hostile to activity in the world than the laxist, modernist, post-Tridentine Catholicism it opposed. Even in the matter of public works and charities such as schools, hospitals, and other similar institutions—a dominant concern of Calvinism and an important aspect of the activity of the Counter-Reformation Church too—the Jansenists were cautious and reserved.[7]

Thus the ideal of irrational effort and labor represented in England and North America by the figure of the "strenuous Puritan" never took root in France. This very failure of religious irrationalism to penetrate the life of the country may go some way toward explaining why the "bourgeois" philosophers of the French Enlightenment made a more strenuous effort than their English counterparts to elaborate a consistent and all-embracing philosophy of man and nature for the new age.[8]

Nearly all the founders of modern thought—and notably of modern political theory—have been pessimists. From Machiavelli to Hobbes reason and nature, power and justice have seemed to be strangers. Descartes is unusual in that his optimism is both fundamental and far-reaching. It lies less in the belief that we can adapt to nature better by understanding her ways, or in the hope that a better understanding of men will lead to a more rational social order, than in something more fundamental still—the conviction that man is in harmony with nature, that the laws governing man are in harmony with those that govern nature, that, in short, the good life is "natural" to man.[9] This aspect of Cartesianism lived on in the minds of the philosophers of the Enlightenment and they inherited a number of problems from it. We shall therefore pause to consider Descartes briefly before going on to the *philosophes* themselves.

Descartes rejected Thomist finalism as vigorously as any Calvinist. But he did not adopt the consequences that other thinkers deduced from their altered conception of the relations between man and the world and between the world and God, namely, that the moral life can be lived only by a few persons through divine grace (Calvinism and to some extent Jansenism), or that it becomes possible only through a reduction of the demands it makes on the individual (Molinism), or that it involves withdrawal from the world (neo-Stoicism). Against all these positions, Descartes affirmed the possibility of a natural virtue, compatible with enjoyment of the good things of this world and of such general application that it could become the constitutive principle of a social order. The way Descartes argues his case is diametrically opposed to Saint Thomas. Unity and harmony are not immediately evident to him. On the contrary, like all the moderns, his immediate experience is of disharmony in the world and alienation from it, and he has to show, therefore, that this world of experience is *not* the real world, that man, likewise, is not really as he appears immediately to the senses and that the "real" world is both intelligible to man and in harmony with him as he "really" is.

Before Descartes, optimism had been generally a mode of thought found in conservative or aristocratic social groups, and the bourgeoisie had tended on the whole to account for itself through pessimistic philosophies, in which the relation of modern (bourgeois) man and the universe (including society) was seen as one of opposition and of conflict (Calvin, Hobbes). Cartesianism offered the prospect of a bourgeois optimism. Such an optimism was possible, however, only within an idealist framework, for it rested on a tremendous abstraction—the reduction of the self, of the person, to pure thinking, and it achieved the harmonization of man and society, man and nature, part and whole, in thought only, and not in fact.

In general Descartes accepted the idealism required by his optimism. The self is defined by the *cogito*—as thinking substance—while the world is mathematized and thus rendered in principle penetrable by the human intellect. In the pure rationality of the self and the pure rationality of the external world, man and the world are reconciled. Thus Descartes maintained the radical distinction between self and world that he shared with nearly all the post-Scholastics, and expressed it in his fundamental distinction between extension or matter and thought; and at the same time he reunited them. The fundamental distinction between spirit and matter tended, however, to devolve into a purely formal or modal distinction. For if matter is fully intelligible, there can be nothing in it that is foreign to thought; matter thus becomes thought "in a material mode." Spinoza was only a logical Cartesian when he affirmed the identity of thought and being and reduced Descartes's two substances to one.

Descartes, however, could not and would not accept this consequence of his attempt to reconcile thought and being, for the idea of the immediate unity of thought and being leads to quietism and is incompatible with the modern goal of the conquest of "material" nature, which Descartes fully espoused. Cartesian optimism, in short, posits a resolution of the antagonism of man and the world (in the sense both of the physical world and of the equally alien social world) and Descartes's philosophy requires in consequence the rationality of both; at the same time, however, Cartesian optimism must include the goal of the conquest of nature by man, the realization as well as the discovery of order, with the result that man and nature have also to be recognized as distinct and even opposite.

These contradictory requirements of Cartesian thought point to the key role in the Cartesian system of God. While Spinoza's unity of thought and being is a self-enclosed system, the question of what guarantees the correspondence of thought with an essentially foreign being is a real one for Descartes. Among several of his followers it was resolved by a *deus ex machina* (occasionalism of Malbranche or preestablished harmony of Leibniz). In Descartes's own philosophy the *deus ex machina* brought in to resolve the problems of the system itself reflected these problems in a new light.

A significant aspect of the relationship of self and world is the question of man's freedom to act in and on the world. Spinoza resolved this question neatly. The rational self cannot be free in the Molinist sense, he held, (that is, undetermined, not subject to law); it is free in that it is self-determined, determined, that is, by reason. Its freedom is realized when it becomes aware of its rational character and of its oneness with a rational world. To Descartes, on the other hand, the separation of the self and the world, the discrepancy between our willing and its object, remain always immediately evident.

My will is so vast, Descartes declares in the *Fourth Meditation,* that I cannot conceive of a vaster one, so much so, indeed, that it is principally my will which lets me know that the image of the divine is in me. Descartes is not thinking of freedom of the will as absolute indifference any more than Spinoza is. He has in mind the endlessness of the will, its transcendence of all objects. To Saint Thomas man is a qualitatively well-defined creature with specific ends that determine the range of his willing. He is free in his choice of the means to those predetermined ends. Descartes's self—and this is surely a characteristic of man as he emerges in the modern world—is, on the other hand, abstract, undefined, endless. And this, precisely, defines his lack of freedom. In the very heyday of the Enlightenment Rousseau drove this point home when he denounced the slavery brought on by boundless desire and called for a reduction of desire to definable, "natural" goals. To revert to such a position, however, would have been contrary to Descartes's whole philosophical endeavor. He therefore accepted that freedom of the will must mean the correspondence of the will with the whole scope of its willing, that is with the infinite universe, and as the correspondence of a finite being with an infinite one is a contradiction, the limit of man's freedom lies in the very limitlessness of his will. "Enfin il faut reconnaître l'infirmité et la faiblesse de notre nature," he writes at the end of the *Meditations.* In principle, then, the will is free; in practice, it is caught in an endless striving toward freedom, that is, toward its own fulfillment in the infinite universe. It is thus constantly realizing its freedom without ever attaining it.

The progressive attainment of freedom is in fact identical with the progressive harmonization of self and world. The harmony of self and world, in short, is *postulated* by Descartes. Correspondingly, instead of being affirmed as present in an immanent God, in whom self and world are one, it is projected onto a transcendent, personal God.

God in Descartes's philosophy is not simply the guarantor of the unity of thought and being. It is through him that the unity of thought and being, on which Descartes's whole conception of the moral life rests, is actually experienced. For the majority of men he is doubtless only the guarantor of the justice of irrational moral commands; for the *sage,* the "philosopher," however, he is the being who is truly free, in whom will and rational necessity are identical. God, according to Descartes, is in a sense man's "true" nature. "I must not imagine that I do not conceive infinity through a real idea, but only through the negation of the finite . . . since, on the contrary, I see manifestly that more reality is found in infinite substance than in finite substance, and consequently that I have the notion of the infinite in me before that of the finite, that is to say the notion of God before the notion of my own self."[10] God, though man's "true" nature, is, however, an ideal, unattainable goal, approached in an endless progress, but never encountered. "Since our knowledge seems able to grow by degree to infinity, and since God's knowledge, being infinite, is already at the point toward which ours is striving, if we consider nothing else, we might be extravagant enough to wish to be gods."[11]

Descartes's solution of the antagonism of man and the world could take only one of two forms: either complete abstraction of all the concrete modalities of being (Spinoza's solution), or projection of the solution onto an infinitely distant point in the future toward which man can strive. Thus Descartes outlines an idea of progress, which, though purely metaphysical in his own thinking, acquired a more concrete significance at the hands of those who came after him.

In Descartes the projected unity of antinomies in God remains strikingly ideal. (Indeed, the arguments for the existence of God—notably the preference for the ontological argument over the teleological one—reveal his place in the Cartesian system more effectively than they demonstrate his existence.) Nicolas Cusanus had earlier argued that man's endless dissatisfaction points to his higher and purer nature, but he believed this higher and purer nature could actually be experienced by the few in mystical ecstasy. By Descartes' time the separation of man and the world, of soul and body, had become so deep that mystical experience had come to be regarded with suspicion. We are too easily deceived, it was held, by the body, the senses, the imagination, our whole "corrupt" nature. How then is the unity of body and soul, of the world and of thought, which Cartesian optimism posits as ultimately real, to be found and known? It can in fact only be known at an intellectual level. And here we discover once again the fundamental antinomies of Cartesian optimism at the very point where they were supposed to be resolved. In mystical ecstasy subjective experience and intellect are bound together. But a passion limited to the pure intellect, an *amor intellectualis Dei,* is a contradiction in terms. Descartes's proof, indeed, appeals to a concrete inner experience (of imperfection) but manages to derive from it only a shadowy and abstract answer. What the ontological proof expresses very clearly is that ardent longing for God (that is, for reconciliation, harmony, and so on) is indeed still a living and experienced reality, but not God himself. Despite the optimism of Descartes, his God is as *absconditus* as Pascal's, an intellectually contrived deduction from an actual experience of loss. Descartes himself declared that the love of God becomes a passion not indeed through our being able to "imagine anything that is in God, who is the object of our love," but through our being able to "imagine our love itself, which consists in our wanting to be united with some object, that is to say, in relation to God, to consider ourselves as a very small part of the vast immensity of things which he has created."[12]

Thus, even for Descartes, what is vividly real is alienation and separation—of soul from world, of man from society—and man's lament at this alienation. Out of this lament, however, comes a desire for reconciliation and totality, for the unity of the part and the whole. In the end Descartes can express this unity and totality only as a kind of regulative idea, an ever-receding goal lying at the end of infinite progress. But it remains a dominant category of his entire thinking and one that the eighteenth-century Enlighteners, impatient of "systems" and eager to attack particular practical problems as they may have been, were not to lose sight of.

## LOCKE AND THE EARLY ENLIGHTENMENT IN FRANCE

Nevertheless, Descartes came under a cloud in the eighteenth century, together with all other authors of metaphysical "systems"—that is, explanations that do not resolve in practice the problems they claim to resolve in theory. Descartes himself had been a man of the *robe,* the highly cultured and leisured cream of the bourgeoisie which, in the sixteenth and seventeenth centuries, had increasingly come to constitute a sort of elite class on its own. The practical-minded, freedom-seeking bourgeoisie of the eighteenth century found his metaphysical idealism at once too speculative and too authoritarian. It became common to dismiss Descartes's philosophy as a chimera or fiction. "Un roman ingénieux," Voltaire, fresh from his trip to England, pronounced.[13]

The French philosophers of the Enlightenment turned instead to Locke and to English empiricism. The renunciation of total metaphysical systems, they observed, had permitted a more fruitful investigation of limited areas of knowledge. The brilliant successes of Newton in physics and astronomy were contrasted with the sterility of Cartesian speculative thought in the same areas. (The opposition of Newton and Descartes was one of the great commonplaces of the first half of the century.) After the mid-century, however, French thinkers tended increasingly to develop the ideas of Locke and the English school in directions that the latter neither foresaw nor approved. In the hands of Helvétius and d'Holbach English sensationalism was transformed into a form of materialism. At the same time the Cartesian enterprise was taken up again on a materialist basis. But the eighteenth-century philosophers were to discover that they could not transcend the alternatives that had already faced Descartes. The materialism that they were developing as a new bourgeois philosophy in competition with officially supported or theologically inspired doctrines was, as we shall see shortly, basically pessimistic. The work of some of the leading philosophes of the second half of the century was in fact marked by a constant and unsuccessful struggle to transcend the limits of both optimistic idealism and pessimistic materialism.

The first half of the eighteenth century was more concerned to attack the idealism and "irrelevance" of the great metaphysical systems of the preceding age than to build a new philosophical system. True, a number of materialist texts, sometimes of Spinozist inspiration, date from this period, but they themselves were speculative on the whole, rather than scientific, and they were in any case not widely disseminated until a later generation of materialists brought them out of the clandestine circuit onto the open market. The atheist and materialist tradition seems moreover to have been characteristic at this time of aristocratic circles—those of the comte de Boulainviller, for instance, or the comte de Plélo—rather than of bourgeois ones.[14] Implying, as it did, both rejection of the divine-right doctrine (on which the theory of absolutism was based) and a kind of quietistic resignation to the course of events, a conquering by "understanding," materialism may have acted as a form of opposition for a depoliticized class. Doubtless too the sexual libertinage that was rife in aristocratic circles and that seems to have taken the place of the traditional heroism and gallantry of the free nobility was at least more compatible with a superficially understood materialism than with Christian morality. There is one known case of materialist atheism that is deeply hostile to the aristocracy. It was the work of a relatively obscure but remarkable parish priest, Jean Meslier. The very vehemence of Meslier's materialism, and in particular of his rejection of civil society, is, however, characteristic of a profoundly religious man, rather than of an urbane and practical eighteenth-century bourgeois.

On the whole, therefore, although there was a certain Spinozistic and speculative philosophical current in the first half of the eighteenth century, the more common tendency of this time was antimetaphysical. Locke had refrained from pronouncing about ultimate reality and this reticence endeared him to the philosophes of the early eighteenth century. Having shown how we come to have the notion of material and spiritual substance—"the one being supposed to be (without knowing what it is) the substratum to those simple ideas we have from without; and the other supposed (with a like ignorance of what it is) to be the substratum to those operations which we experiment in ourselves within"—he concludes guardedly that "from our not having any notion of the substance of spirit, we can no more conclude its nonexistence than we can, for the same reason, deny the existence of body."[15] The whole matter of the "secret and abstract nature of substance in general" is quite simply abandoned as otiose. Locke concentrates his attention not on the nature of things but on the nature of knowing. Voltaire faithfully followed his master of many years: "Ce mot même de *substance, ce qui est dessous,* nous avertit assez que ce dessous nous sera inconnu à jamais: quelque chose que nous découvrions de ses apparences, il restera toujours ce dessous à découvrir."[16] At the end of *Micromégas* the secretary of the Academy of Sciences —the Cartesian Fontenelle—opens with trembling hands the great book in which he hopes that his interplanetary friend will have communicated *le fond des choses,* to find that it is perfectly blank. The alpha and omega of things is thus unknown to us. Between the knowing subject (the self) and the object of his knowing (nature, the world) there is not that correspondence or harmony which Descartes worked so hard to prove, but an unbridgeable gulf. What men can have is thus not knowledge of the way things are but "useful" knowledge—working systematizations of separate areas of experience without knowledge of the whole. Locke himself was happy enough with this kind of knowledge, which is available to us "dans ce cercle étroit où nous sommes enfermés," as Voltaire put it.[17] Indeed to him the circle did not appear so narrow, and it was to the many mansions of the practical sciences that he—and Voltaire for the most part—directed his attention and that of his readers. Why should we be concerned with what we cannot know or seek to create a total and unified system of knowledge, which will in the end turn out to be illusory? Why can we not accept that there are many spheres of practical knowledge and get on with finding out what we can know in each? The very fact that where knowledge is useful to us, we can discover it, is itself indeed a proof of the benevolence and intelligence of the supreme Watchmaker: "The infinite wise Contrivor of us and all things about us hath fitted our senses, faculties, and organs to the conveniences of life, and the business we have to do here. We are able, by our senses, to know and distinguish things, and to examine them so far as to apply them to our uses, and several ways to accommodate the exigencies of this life. We have insight enough into their admirable contrivances and wonderful effects to admire and magnify the wisdom, power, and goodness of their Author. Such a knowledge as this, which is suited to our present condition, we want not faculties to attain. But it appears not that God intended we should have a perfect, clear, and adequate knowledge of them: that perhaps is not in the comprehension of any finite being. We are furnished with faculties (dull and weak as they are) to discover enough in the creatures to lead us to knowledge of the Creator and the knowledge of our duty, and we are fitted well enough with abilities to provide for the conveniences of living: these are our business in this world."[18] Or, as Voltaire counseled more tersely in a famous phrase: "Il faut cultiver notre jardin."

Locke's outlook could have seemed attractive to several important groups in eighteenth-century French society—to the active and enterprising part of the bourgeoisie, eager not to revolutionize the whole fabric of society, but to get on with its own job within it; to the royal administration, which also had to deal with practical problems and wished to be able to do so with as little obstruction as possible from theological and ecclesiastical sources; and even to the church and the aristocracy. A great deal of Locke's appeal to eighteenth-century Frenchmen may indeed have been due to the fact that he could be interpreted as providing a legitimation of "modern" science, "modern" values, and "modern" life in general, without *directly* attacking the traditional bases on which the general framework of authority rested. His philosophy seemed to allow for peaceful coexistence in mutual tolerance (or indifference) of God and man, faith and reason, poetry and prose, church and state, authority and individual freedom, public conventions and private fantasies, the "ancient" and the "modern." At least it discouraged direct and potentially dangerous confrontations.

Post-Tridentine Catholicism had made important concessions to the world of the absolutist prince, of *raison d'état,* and of mercantilism. *Realpolitik* and commercial enterprise were after all facts of modern life in France as well as in England, and both the state and individuals did in fact pursue policies of self-interest that had little or nothing to do with divinely instituted ends. Since it could not alter this situation, the church sought rather to accommodate it while at the same time trying to influence, to the best of its ability, the policies of princes and the practices of private persons. The moral theory of post-Tridentine Catholicism allows for areas of "neutral" activity, areas in which man is free to pursue his own autonomous ends, provided he does not transgress God's commands in so doing. The world of human action thus looks like a map in which "free" zones (*adiaphora*) are marked out by lines that it is prohibited to cross. Sin in this scheme of things was not so much a mark of man's corrupt nature since the Fall—an aspect of his whole being, ever present in all his thought and action until cleared by grace—as a specific act, encountered, as it were, from time to time, on those occasions when the individual came up against and transgressed external lines of demarcation. Likewise, although divine Providence was by no means denied in post-Tridentine thought, it might be likened to a *commedia dell'arte* scenario in which the actors enjoy a great deal of freedom to improvise within an established framework. Such a doctrine was clearly useful to princes, courtiers, and even libertines, eager to obtain maximum freedom without actually breaking with the church, and it was strongly opposed for this reason by moral rigorists and by many who disliked both the court and the wealthy court aristocracy. But it also allowed, in a limited way, for the development of the sciences, and of activities and ways of thought that were independent of and "irrelevant" to religion.

The areas of freedom were charted within a general framework, over which the church retained its jurisdiction in principle, but which could in a sense be ignored as long as one's acts or ideas were limited to the area in question and did not spill out beyond it. The pursuit of pleasure and money, natural science, economics, politics, and literature was thus allowable to some extent without reference to an overall divine plan, on condition that it did not reach out toward totalization, that is towards an explicitly new view of man and the world. Unlike Calvinism, post-Tridentine Catholicism did not invest labor with a religious value and it did not turn activity in the world into a form of religious asceticism. It did not therefore actually *encourage* practical worldly activity. But it did at least tolerate such activity as well as the kind of intellectual inquiry that accompanies and guides it.

The philosophy of Locke was in some important respects more compatible with the new moral and epistemological position of the church than Cartesianism. Eschewing total systems and leaving aside "unanswerable" questions concerning ultimate reality, Locke had left a space which could be filled by theology. To be sure, he had emphasized the worldly rather than the otherworldly, action rather than meditation, appearance rather than "reality," and he had removed God and spiritual affairs in general, by implication at least, to the periphery of man's social preoccupations—or to the personal fantasy world of each individual—but he had not confronted the church with a clearly rival philosophy. Since he made no claim to speak of the total nature of things as it is in "reality" and, indeed, affirmed that as a philosopher he could not do so, he did not actually attack the theologians. The Lockean philosopher could only say that by his criteria what the theologian said made no sense.

In its struggle both with the pessimistic Jansenists who intransigently opposed all attempts to compromise with the world—that is, make it easier for Christians to come to terms with it and follow its ways—and with Cartesianism which, though associated with and taught by Oratorians and Jansenists, was a basically optimistic philosophy, the church may have found in Locke a useful, if temporary ally. The official church accepted neither the difficult tensions of Jansenism nor the Cartesian resolution of these. It clung precariously to a doctrine that attempted to reconcile a limited valuation of nature and this world with the reality of Original Sin and the Fall. For reasons which C. B. Macpherson has clarified, Locke's social philosophy also attempted to reconcile two conceptions of nature, one pessimistic and the other optimistic, one basically Hobbesian and the other affirming that the state of nature is a state of peaceful and harmonious social life.[19] It is certainly striking that the Jesuits—the most powerful force in the post-Tridentine church and the most zealous enemies of Cartesianism—refrained for some time from attacking Locke or, indeed, the *Modernes* in general with the vehemence one might have expected.[20]

The reformed eighteenth-century aristocracy also found much that was pleasing in Locke's individualism and sensationalism: specifically, arguments against absolutism and "despotism," which did not, however, extend to complete subversion of the established principles of political authority, but rather justified the subordination of the masses to the government of a select group, and, more generally, a system of thought that could be adapted to support its own values and way of life.

Alienated from its former social and political functions, the aristocracy of Louis XIV and his successors—together with part of the leisured bourgeoisie—was lost without its *divertissements,* intellectual, aesthetic, or erotic. A large part of this class seems to have experienced itself as a kind of inertia or vacancy, a tabula rasa, which could be given form and consistency only by some external stimulus. To exist, for it, was, characteristically, not to think or even to do, but to feel, and life for many of its members was a constant pursuit of the varying stimuli necessary to maintain oneself in existence, a constant flight from the ever present danger of *ennui,* with its accompanying languor and loss of the sense of being. In the paintings of Watteau there are figures whose empty faces and listless bodies convey something of this inertia, others whose looks are turned towards an ideal Elsewhere, dimly perceived at the end of a long avenue, others still whose greedy gaze is directed towards that which animates it, the object of desire. Always it is outside the self that the source of life is seen to reside. "Nous restons là comme des eaux dormantes, qui attendent qu'on les remue pour remuer," says Marivaux's Lélio.[21]

Moreover, if the soul is not to fall back into its original vacancy and stupor, the stimuli must be constantly varied. The early eighteenth century is the age par excellence of the detail that delights and of the novel twist that surprises an expectation. The whole aesthetic theory of the Modernes is in fact based on variety, the playful and decorative application and modification of a repertoire of forms that has become wearisome and dull. In a passage that reads like a defense of the Modernes and the so-called "petit goût" against the *Anciens* and the "grand goût," Montesquieu justifies the principle of variety in the arts. "The soul cannot sustain for long the same situations. . . . Everything wearies us in the end, especially great pleasures: we leave them with as much satisfaction as we took them; for the fibers that are the organs of those pleasures have to be relaxed; we must put others, which are more ready to work for us, into service, and spread the load, so to speak. Our soul is weary of sensation; but to be without sensation is to fall into a depression that crushes it completely. There is a remedy for it all in moving constantly among the various modifications of the soul; in this way it feels but does not weary."[22]

The ideas expressed by the writers of the early eighteenth century do not simply "reflect" the feelings of a certain social class. They also project an original view of man as a social and worldly creature incomprehensible apart from others and dependent on society for his very humanity. It may even be that such a view of man—as existing through his relations with others rather than as a substantial, self-contained entity—could best take root in a class whose life revealed most abstractly and in its purest form, so to speak, the social nature of man. Nevertheless, this particular view of the social nature of man bears a class imprint in the striking fact that any reference to the principal social activity of the vast majority of men—work—is absent from it. Thus the "aristocratic" interpretation of Locke fastened on certain aspects of his thought rather than on others—on sensation itself, for instance, seen as a justification of the life of pleasure, rather than on the active work of reflection by which, according to Locke, man transforms the data of the senses. Understood in a certain way, therefore, both Locke's sensationalism and his individualism could be welcomed by an aristocracy dedicated to the social pleasures and newly emancipated, as far as its private life was concerned, from the "tyranny" of Versailles. It is not an accident, surely, that Locke was a popular philosopher in the society of salons which developed during and after the Regency.

For various reasons, therefore, the dominant strata of French society in the early eighteenth century were receptive to the philosophy of Locke and increasingly disinterested in Cartesianism and its problems. Indeed, in many ways Locke's empiricism provided a meeting ground for "aristocratic" and "bourgeois" Enlighteners, for those to whom Enlightenment meant above all freedom to enjoy without the constraint of myths and outworn rules and for those to whom it meant rather freedom to create without such constraint, to those to whom it meant a resumption of rights and to those to whom it meant an assumption of rights. In the first half of the century the difference between the goals and values of the various groups that were critical of the regime were not clearly apparent. It was in the second half of the century that these differences gradually led to divisions within the camp of the Enlighteners themselves, the most advanced of them pushing toward an all-encompassing materialism that would undermine the foundations of tradition and authority far more thoroughly than the philosophy of Locke or of Voltaire.

## THE HIGH ENLIGHTENMENT:
## MATERIALISM AND OPTIMISM

Political historians, literary historians, art historians, and economic historians are all agreed that there was a turning point in eighteenth-century social, economic, and intellectual life somewhere around the mid-century. It was in fact at a time of growing prosperity and growing impatience with restrictions of all sorts that the generation of Rousseau, Diderot, Helvétius, and d'Holbach came into its own. The small elitist circles of the early eighteenth century were now enlarged and *philosophie* emerged from the salon to enter the marketplace and the public reading room. The older generation itself altered its tactics if not its long-term goals or its fundamental values, turning from ironical gibes to large-scale campaigns to mobilize public opinion (for example, Voltaire's activities on behalf of Calas, Sirven, and other victims of judicial abuses). In the history of ideas this turning point is marked by the increasingly aggressive materialism of the philosophes, which was itself in part a response to renewed militancy on the part of the church, the parlements and the royal power itself.[23] Coexistence seemed less and less possible, and the philosophes undertook not simply to weaken the ideological defenses of the traditional sources of authority but to subvert them altogether. Not only Orthodoxy but deism itself came under increasingly heavy fire from a total philosophy of nature with no room in it for any "spiritual" forces or transcendental principle of authority whatever, not even the Supreme Watchmaker.

A certain confusion over the concept of nature—seen both as that which is and as that which ought to be, as fact and norm—is found in a great deal of the political, ethical, and aesthetic thought of the seventeenth and eighteenth centuries. This confusion was encouraged by the success of Newtonian physics. Newton had revealed a physical universe that was admirably governed by laws, a marvelous mechanism comparable to, yet infinitely surpassing, the creation of the most skillful watchmaker. How not to believe that such a universe was the result of a deliberate plan by a divine legislator, that the laws of nature reveal an order willed by God, and that ours is thus the best of all possible worlds? For man the task must be to discover this marvelous order in his own sphere—the laws of ethics, aesthetics, politics—to publish it in a new (and true) revelation, and to clear away whatever dirt and debris might be clogging the works, obstructing the smooth functioning of the mechanism. It was only too easy to argue correspondingly that the order of society itself was as marvelous as that of nature. There were doubtless some "imperfections" that ought to be removed, but the social world as a whole, like the physical world, could be thought of as representing the best of possible worlds, the optimum degree of order and harmony compatible with individuality and freedom. Eighteenth-century deism was thus not simply a religious attitude or a scientific one. It had social implications and it was in many ways a comprehensive ideology.

In England deism might possibly be considered the consecration of the social and political order achieved by the Glorious Revolution of 1688. In France it was inevitably more combative and it tended to be championed by those who wished reforms. Nevertheless, French deism too, if it implied rejection of the authority of the church, also implied continued acceptance of an authority principle transcending the body politic itself and sustaining social order.

By thoroughly demystifying nature, materialism removed the last vestige of transcendental authority and control. At the same time, materialism was incompatible with a form of positivism that was frequently associated with Locke and Newton and that fitted easily into the deistic framework. As we saw earlier, Locke could be interpreted as implying that what we know, our scientific knowledge, is an ordering and structuring of our sense experience. As such, it is adequate for the practical conduct of our lives and indeed the fact that it is enough confirms the skill and benevolence with which God has fitted out his universe. We do not know or need to know if it properly "reflects" reality.

But if our knowledge is simply adequate to our needs, there is, in principle at least, an unbridgeable gulf between the known and knowable on the one hand and the unknown and unknowable on the other. To a materialist such as Diderot, however, the space between the known and the unknown did not separate two disparate universes, one of which was an object of empirical investigation, while the other was not. It was simply the distance between the partial understanding of man and the total understanding ("la langue philosophique complète") toward which he is constantly striving. "When we compare the infinite multitude of natural phenomena with the limits of our understanding and the weakness of our powers of perception," Diderot wrote, "how can we expect from slow and laborious studies, which are interrupted at frequent intervals and for long periods at a time, and from a tiny handful of truly creative geniuses, more than a few broken and isolated pieces of the great chain that links all things together? . . . When will the philosophical language be perfected? And if it were, which individual man, among men, could know it? If the Eternal, wishing to manifest his omnipotence even more clearly than through the wonders of nature, had deigned to unfold on paper and in his own hand the workings of the universe, does it seem likely that this great book would be more intelligible to us than the universe itself?"[24]

Diderot's scepticism derives not from any idea that there is a realm that is unknowable, but from his awareness of the problems involved in the part's knowing the ongoing whole of which it is a living part, and from a questioning of the very notion of knowledge as a kind of "tableau" or "representation" of reality in the mind. In a world of constant change, as he was coming to see it, how could things be regarded as fixed, and if they were not as fixed as the words that represent them, if it was impossible to grasp the continuum of reality in classifications and languages that are necessarily discontinuous, how could the "langue philosophique" be constructed? "Si l'état des êtres est dans une vicissitude perpétuelle; si la nature est encore à l'ouvrage, . . . il n'y a point de philosophie. Toute notre science naturelle devient aussi transitive que les mots."[25] A significant part of Diderot's work—beginning as early as his translation of the English neo-Platonist Shaftesbury, a curious and indicative choice for the young Diderot to have made—consists, in effect, of an exploration and undermining of the apparently solid conceptual and linguistic categories with which many of his contemporaries tried to encompass the real world of nature. And to the degree that reason and knowledge for him are not fixed but evolving, the collective enterprise of many men and many generations, he almost invariably chose to write in the form of the dialogue with multiple voices, conscious and even unconscious, interpolated dreams, flights of imaginative speculation, anecdotes, aphorisms, paradoxes, and digressions. His own idea of reason as process and collective effort must have seemed to him to be better caught in this kind of writing than in the philosophical treatise.

Diderot's scepticism, in sum, concerned the very idea of knowledge current among his contemporaries rather than the ideal of the unity of knowledge, which they were willing to give up, but which he continued to share with Descartes even though he interpreted it differently from his predecessor. "Sans l'idée de tout, plus de philosophie," he wrote.[26] But the exploration of nature, which is identical with the elaboration of a total philosophy, can only be a collective task, in his view, that men carry out over the centuries, and that will never be complete. Nor will any one man ever be able to embrace the whole of human knowledge in the eaglelike view that was the goal of Cartesian science: "What, then, is our goal? The execution of a work that can never be completed and that would be far beyond human intelligence to comprehend if it were completed. Are we not madder than the first inhabitants of the plain of Sennaar? We know that from the earth to the sky the distance is infinite, yet we do not cease from building the tower."[27] Knowledge, in Diderot's view, comes to be similar to a language, constantly growing and changing, the creation of human society in the course of its collective history, rather than the property of single individuals, a totality of possibilities always beyond the reach of any single user of it.

The debate between deists and materialists involved far-reaching ideological positions, but it was also closely related to developments in the sciences. The *je* or narrative persona of the *Pensées philosophiques* of 1746, for instance, is a deist and he justifies his position on the grounds that the theory of spontaneous generation had been discredited by the experiments of modern students of mechanistic biology, such as Redi and Leeuwenhoek: "Natural philosophy has had the privilege of making the first true deists. With the discovery of germ cells alone, one of the most powerful arguments of the atheists has been destroyed. Whether motion be accidental to matter or essential to it, I am now convinced that its effects do not go beyond the development of what already exists;[28] all the evidence concurs in demonstrating to me that putrefaction in itself can produce no organized matter."[29] If spontaneous generation is ruled out, and the more up-to-date preformationist theory (or theory of *emboîtement,* as it was called) seems better to account for the facts, then there is an original order or model that determines the form of all existing matter. Time is simply the unfolding or realization of a preestablished design. As Fontenelle put it: "Ainsi toutes ces fleurs ne feraient que se développer à l'infini les unes dedans les autres; et ce qu'on appelle générations ne seraient plus des formations nouvelles, mais des développements."[30] Diderot's progressive rejection of deism coincided likewise with his progressive rejection of the preformationist theory in biology. "Vous ne croyez donc pas aux germes préexistants," the character d'Alembert asks in the *Entretien,* written in the 1760s. "Non," the character Diderot answers unhesitatingly.

Tied as it was to developments in the scientific domain, however, the implications of deism far transcended it. The preformationist theory in biology was important not only to deism conceived as an answer to a scientific problem, but to the whole idea of a fixed order of things transcendentally rooted in the divine intellect and will. As such it was defended zealously by the champions of this idea of order. Voltaire's unceasing attacks on Needham (whose work, around the mid-century, supported a revival of the spontaneous generation and transformationist theories) are mostly understandable as a defense of a stable, transcendentally ordered, natural and social world. Between 1768 and 1772, in a series of minor and major writings, Voltaire poured scorn on the "jésuite irlandais imbécile qui a cru faire des anguilles avec de la farine"[31] and whose ideas had seduced many otherwise sensible people, including a number of "philosophers." (Among them Voltaire might have numbered Diderot, d'Holbach, Maupertuis, Buffon, and Lagrange, the editor of Lucretius.) Voltaire was right, as it happens, to be suspicious of Needham, but the ideological bias of his argument is unmistakable. The fortunes of materialism, as Voltaire knew, are not exclusively tied to Needham; Voltaire, however, infers that they are. His opposition to materialism and to transformationist theories of matter and his loyalty to the deist position were, on his own admission, based on the threat that materialism posed to the idea of a fixed order of things. Needham's biology, he cried, implied that "il n'y avait plus de germes"[32] and if this was indeed so, "voilà toute la nature bouleversée."[33]

What the materialists thus increasingly questioned was the assumption that matter or nature was incapable of organizing itself, that it had required a "divine architect" to put it in motion, give it the order it has, and maintain it in that order—even if the maintenance was limited to occasional adjustments, as with Newton. In a speculative way Diderot had long been pondering this question. "Parce que je ne conçois pas comment le mouvement a pu engendrer cet univers, qu'il a si bien la vertu de conserver, il est ridicule de lever cette difficulté par l'existence supposée d'un être que je ne conçois pas davantage," he lets an atheist interlocutor say in the *Pensées philosophiques*. The story of the tortoise supporting the world, which Locke had used to lay bare the "myth" of substance—and which Diderot had found again in Shaftesbury—was thus taken over by Diderot as an argument against transcendental reality in general, and against the notion of the prime mover in particular. As such, it recurs again and again in his work.[34] The problem of linking the divine spirit to its creation revealed, according to d'Holbach, what a poor solution the Divine Architect was. Invoking it, one simply traded a clear difficulty for a mess of mystifications, "ingénieuses chimères  .  .  .  de *l'harmonie préétablie,* des *causes occasionnelles,* de la *prémotion physique,* etc."[35]

The great central scene of the death of Saunderson in Diderot's *Lettre sur les aveugles,* prudently flanked though it is by discussions of more technical problems of philosophy, is a bold frontal attack on the argument from design, the principal basis of deism. "Imagine,  .  .  .  if you will," says the dying geometer—and what a stroke of genius to have put these thoughts into the mouth of a geometer, a colleague of Newton, the very rock on which deism rested!—"that the order you find so striking has always existed, but permit me to believe that it has not, that if we could go back to the origin of things and of the ages and could feel matter first begin to move and the chaos start to take shape, we would encounter a multitude of unformed beings and only a few well-organized ones. If I cannot offer arguments against your view of the present state of things, I can at least question your view of their former state. . . . I might inquire, for instance, who told you, Leibniz, Clarke and Newton, that at the time when the first animals took form, there were not some which were headless, others which were without feet? I might argue that some had no stomach and others no intestines; that others again which, possessing a stomach, a palate and teeth, seemed likely to survive, passed out of existence because of some defect of the heart or the lungs; that monstrous creatures have arisen and passed, one after the other, into nothingness; that all the defective organizations of matter have now disappeared, and that only those have survived whose constitution was free of significant contradictions and which were therefore able to subsist unaided and to perpetuate themselves. Supposing you grant me all this, then if the first man had had a blocked larynx or had been unable to find suitable food, or if the organs of generation had been defective in him, or if he had failed to encounter a female partner, or had combined with other species, what then, Mr. Holmes, would have become of the human race? It would have been enveloped in the general depuration of the universe; and the proud creature that calls itself man would have been dissolved and scattered among the molecules of matter, would have remained, perhaps forever, a mere possibility. If there never had been any ill-formed creatures, you would not fail, I know, to claim that there never will be any, and that I am rushing into fanciful hypotheses; but the order of things is not so perfect," Saunderson went on, "that monstrous productions do not occur from time to time even now." Then, turning to face the minister, he added, "Consider me, Mr. Holmes. I have no eyes. What did we do to God, you and I, that one of us should have the organ of sight and the other be deprived of it?"[36]

Saunderson is putting forward a hypothesis borrowed from Lucretius, which he suggests—and the dramatic pathos of this scene carries the reader along—is at least as convincing as that of the deists. Nature is one thing for the hale and the happy, and another for the wretched and the sick, he is saying, and you, the contented ones, are simply reading your own contentment into the universe around you. Your belief in its perfection and stability are simply projections of your own satisfaction with things and desire that they remain as they are, which you then justify in turn by that perfection and stability. Or, as Dom Deschamps expressed it, the order that we read into the universe is the expression of our own submission to civil laws. Men in the state of *moeurs* (that is, after the withering away of the laws, the state, and all other forms of constraint) "sauraient que l'extraordinaire est dans l'ordre des choses, où tout est plus ou moins possible."[37]

Diderot's use of the exceptional and the monstrous to lay bare the cozy and conventional character of the conception of nature most widely admitted by "enlightened" people has obvious—and devastating—implications for aesthetics, morals, and politics as well. Here, however, the materialists themselves ran into difficulties, as we shall see shortly. They held that moral and social order could not be transcendentally grounded; it had to be grounded in nature, understood as an immanent, self-contained system. But what, then, of the "monsters," the madmen, the criminals, the blind? Are they too not part of "nature"? Are there two "natures"—one all a harmony of self-interested and like-minded people, and the other a Hobbesian universe in which equally self-interested but fundamentally disparate people struggle with each other, without understanding or compassion, to the death? The historian might be curious about the social significance of this ambiguity in the term nature. Why is human nature not admitted to be as diverse and as amoral as physical nature? Diderot himself explored this question in several of his most brilliant works, but he refrained, in general, from publishing them in his own lifetime. They would have divided and disturbed the philosophes and Diderot's immediate aim was to rally them.

To the stable, fixed, somewhat abstract mathematical order of the deist universe, the materialists opposed a concrete universe of individuals as well as types, endowed with energy, self-generating, self-sustaining, self-transforming, constantly in process of change—a universe closer to the dreams of the biologist and the chemist than to those of the physicist and the astronomer. Diderot inveighed against the mathematical model of most modern thought and, carried away by his own polemic, rashly predicted its imminent decline.[38] Buffon declared that nature's own movement "more than perpetual, assisted by the perpetuity of time, produces, induces, introduces all possible events, all possible combinations; nature needs neither instruments, nor crucibles, nor the hand of an intelligent being."[39] "I regard organization as an essential quality of matter," Robinet wrote in similar vein. "Organic beings can be divided, broken, mashed up; their form and total structure will be destroyed in this way, but the organization of the parts will not; it cannot be taken from them: as long as they are matter, they remain organic whatever the state they are in, and retain the capacity of providing themselves with nourishment, of growing and of engendering, and this capacity will be deployed as soon as circumstances are favorable."[40]

Many problems remained—was there, as Buffon argued, a radical distinction between a *matière morte* and a *matière vivante?* And if so, was not the unity of nature thereby irreparably fragmented? Diderot takes up this problem in a series of questions at the end of *De l'Interprétation de la nature.* What is striking about his handling of it is that for him it is a scientific problem, not a metaphysical one. Its solution must wait upon the patient research of the scientists. At best, in the meantime, one can make conjectures. Diderot deals in the same way with the question of the species. For Buffon, it seems, as in antiquity for Lucretius, the species were fixed; they were born and they might die out, but there was no movement among them. Diderot, on the other hand, like Maupertuis and Robinet, envisaged the possibility of a single "premier animal prototype de tous les animaux"[41] and even of a gradation through the various realms—the mineral, vegetable, and animal.[42]

Despite hesitancies, inconsistencies, and unresolved problems, almost all eighteenth-century forms of materialism implied rejection not only of a hidden hand that controlled nature from the outside, however rationally it might be conceived to behave, but also of the whole deist conception of a stable universe, whose component parts remained constant and identical with themselves. "Nature . . . cannot persist in the same state," Robinet wrote in 1766. "It changes its form constantly, it has always changed its form . . . If we were to go backward in time through the whole succession of past forms, we would never encounter a first one: there never was one that was not preceded by another. The succession of forms that the world must still assume is likewise inexhaustible."[43] As early as 1753 Diderot had formulated the significance of the new materialist conception of the world: "If all beings undergo successive changes, passing through the most imperceptible nuances, then time, which never stops, must in the end create a vast difference between those forms that existed in the remote past, those that exist today, and those that will exist in the distant future; and then *nil sub sole novum* is only a prejudice based on the weakness of our organs, the imperfection of our instruments of measurement, and the brevity of our lives."[44]

In Voltaire's *Candide* men are compared to the rats in the hold of a ship whose captain is unconcerned about their particular fate. Voltaire thus pinpointed one of the weaknesses of providentialism in its rationalist-deist form—its inability to account for the individual and the concrete. But he left the captain in charge of the ship. The materialist philosophers of the eighteenth century went further than the author of *Candide* in their rejection of providentialism. They denied that the captain existed at all. It was not only the Christian God who was dethroned but the deist God too; and by implication not only the absolutist monarch but the enlightened one also, in so far as he was thought of as ruling according to preestablished laws rather than according to the will of the "people." Nature, as the materialists envisaged it, could no longer be used to legitimate a social order envisaged as essentially unchanging and a form of political authority conceived of as external to the body of the governed itself. The materialist philosophers, in short, had read a far more consistent rejection of authority into their view of nature than the deists had done, and the social philosophy that they deduced back from their view of nature was likewise more consistently opposed to authority and to established forms of society. Just as the source of nature's energy and order for them is immanent in nature herself, so the source of political and social order is immanent in the whole of the body politic.

But if the eighteenth-century materialists had undermined the foundations of political and ecclesiastical authority far more thoroughly than their deist predecessors, they had won a literary or philosophical victory, not a practical one. The category of possibility, the notion that things need not be what they are but might be otherwise, was introduced by Diderot into almost all his writings: in the *Lettre sur les aveugles* the world of the blind undermines the world of those who see; in *Le Neveu de Rameau* the world of Rameau undermines the world of the philosopher *Moi*; in *Jacques le fataliste* the *grand rouleau* of destiny, which constantly turns, encourages the servant's confidence that the master with his stupid belief in his own freedom to impose his will on things—a belief that the novel has already belied—will be proved wrong. Indeed, literature itself might be considered the domain of the possible—since nothing in it *need* be and anything can be otherwise—and in this sense eighteenth-century literature, which was highly self-conscious and aware of its oppositional character, was in its very being a constant subversion of a too solidly established "reality." Meanwhile, however, the kings and the bishops, the upholders of this reality, still sat securely on their thrones and the most anticlerical and antispiritual of the philosophers could not provide a rationale of political and social action to unseat them. Subversion remained theoretical only. Consciousness exhausted its possibilities in the recognition of the constantly changing, self-determining and all-embracing system which nature is; it could not itself affect the course of events. There was in fact no room in the thinking even of the materialist philosophers for the transformation of thought into action and of philosophie into history. Jacques was hopeful and energetic but he was rarely more than a *fataliste*. Moreover, to the degree that some of the materialists substituted an immanent harmony for a transcendentally imprinted and sustained one, they were even more vulnerable than the deists to objections based on the experience of disharmony and conflict. The materialist position risked ending in a double pessimism: concerning the world itself, and concerning the possibility of changing it.

The gulf between reason and nature, consciousness and being, subjectivity and objectivity, which the modern world had dug and which Descartes had both acknowledged and tried to heal, was sidetracked rather than resolved by Locke. Despite the latter's admonitions, however, men continued to be puzzled and disconcerted by an inscrutable nature, which was felt to be both the object of consciousness and a constant affront to it. Consciousness, wit, reason, imagination cannot function without objects; yet the world of objects, which they cannot do without, remains impermeable to them and, indeed, threatens constantly to devour them. For in its efforts to understand itself, consciousness alienates itself, makes itself an object, and finds itself torn between an "objective" account of itself as brain and a "subjective" account of itself as spirit, between itself as knower and itself as known. Voltaire seems to have been haunted by the paradox of man's unbreakable relation to an inscrutable nature which assumes in the writer's imagination, scarcely less than in that of the Protestant, the aspect of sin and corruption. While constantly reminding himself and his readers of their natural origin, he invariably describes the foetus in repulsive terms. And he is distressed not only by gestation and birth, but by all the natural body processes. Not only the natural world, the social world, history itself in its pure positivity is constantly felt by Voltaire as a threat and a kind of insult: he therefore makes it an object of ridicule or, with great effectiveness, he appropriates it, makes it the pretext of a purely human artifact, of the work of literature. By wrenching history out of "reality" and using it to spin stories, Voltaire the writer wins a victory for the mind, for humanity, which, nevertheless, even in the moment of success, recognizes the precariousness of its triumph and its ultimate dependence. The absurdity of George Fox in the *Lettres philosophiques* is the absurdity not only of Christ and the religious "fanatic" in general, but of all historical existence, and in the end it can affect the actively involved philosopher along with the Christian. Not only Charles XII and Peter the Great, these two superheroes of reality, but the philosophers as well— Maupertuis, König, and Voltaire himself—are stripped of their historical reality, of that which makes them necessarily what they are and nothing else, when they are resuscitated as *personæ* in the gratuitous universe of literature.

Resting as they do on an obviously fabulous and imagined base, the *contes* with their constantly shifting perspectives, their conniving ironies, allusions and ceaseless digressions, are deservedly regarded as among the greatest and most characteristic achievements of Voltaire. They are Voltaire's way to freedom and fellowship with others—a fellowship that is understood, incidentally, only in the mode of identity and that can be achieved consequently only in negation of the historically real. In negation, in pure thought, all concrete differences are ironed out and that which might separate and create difference, otherness, is constantly overcome. One can see why Voltaire appealed to people of widely varying interests. The community into which he led them was formed by an intellectual denial of the objective historical reality dividing them: this reality, however, remained in practice intact.

Diderot the materialist does not altogether escape Voltaire's dilemma. He embraces at times a radical objective determinism, based on physiology, which leads in the end to a pessimistic view of man and society. Nor does the noble view of man as the self-consciousness of nature, which he puts forward in the article "Encyclopédie" of the *Encyclopédie* overcome this pessimism. Only in some of his most adventurous writings did Diderot come close to breaking down the barrier between thinking and acting. In the *Rêve de d'Alembert,* for example, consciousness is judged the highest form of organization of nature, and intelligence one of the means by which she fulfills her ends. Likewise, in *Jacques le fataliste* there are a few critical moments when Jacques forgets the grand rouleau and threateningly warns the master that he has it in his power to terminate their relationship at any time. On the whole, however, the materialists remained stuck with the problem of deducing an effective social philosophy, a morality of action from a blindly self-determining nature.

"N'adorons point, ne flattons point à la manière des hommes, une nature sourde qui agit nécessairement et dont rien ne peut déranger le cours," d'Holbach wrote. The very determinism of nature, in short, the absoluteness of her immanent law frees man from his enslavement to false laws and impostures of authority. The actual positive content that nature gives to social and moral laws remains somewhat vague, however; and it is never clear if they are descriptive or prescriptive, if they describe what we do and cannot help doing or what we ought to do and may do. We should find out, d'Holbach says, what the true laws of our nature are—below the habits formed by "superstition" and a false culture—and follow them. In this way we shall make ourselves happy and work for the good of society; for those who refuse to be what they are and to follow the laws of nature will be "infailliblement punis par les erreurs sans nombre dont notre esprit se trouverait aveuglé, et dont les maux sans nombre seraient les suites nécessaires."[45] The pursuit by each of his own properly understood natural end does not involve conflict or disharmony, because, all men being similarly structured, the desires of each and the desires of all, the interest of the one and the interest of the many, properly understood, are identical. The disappearance of the guiding hand, in short, does not appear to have affected d'Holbach's basic optimism about nature.

This optimism was not shared by everybody, however. Even the older—and in some ways more easily defensible—deistic optimism had not ceased to be questioned, often by men with strong Protestant or at least Augustinian backgrounds. Thus the writings of the Physiocrats, which expressed the optimism of the propertied classes during the boom years of the second third of the century and advocated a policy of laissez faire or complete confidence in the divinely established "natural" order of things, drew upon themselves a great deal of criticism, which ultimately affected the whole idea of the unity and harmony of nature. The Utopian Mably,[46] the finance minister Necker,[47] and the journalist Linguet,[48] among others, questioned the Physiocrats' efforts to justify social and economic liberalism on the grounds that it realizes the "natural order" of economics and of society. "Society is far from being a perfect work," Necker wrote; "and there is very little cause for us to consider the different relations we observe around us, especially that common contrast of power and weakness, slavery and authority, wealth and misfortune, luxury and miserable poverty, as forming an harmonious composition; so many inequalities, so many varie-gated characteristics cannot possibly constitute an edifice of impressively just proportions."[49] According to Linguet, men had been better off as slaves than they were as free workers. To the descendants of the slaves of anti-quity freedom means only the right to die of starvation. The master of old had some interest in the well-being of his slaves, at least as much interest as the eighteenth-century farmer had in his workhorses, since both repre-sented a capital investment. The free worker, however, has no influence over his master, since he is always replaceable at no cost. "He is free, you say; ah! that is his misfortune. He is bound to no one, but no one is bound to him either  . . .  Dayworkers are born, raised, and prepared for the service of opulence, at absolutely no cost to the latter, like the game it massacres on its estates."[50]

Neither the Protestant Necker nor Linguet, the son of an ardent Jansenist, thought that the social order could be essentially altered. Pro-perty, the basis of the social order, was here to stay. Both argued therefore not for the free play of the market, but for government controls and restric-tions, designed to palliate the evils of the market and to protect the poor from the rich, the weak from the strong.

Diderot himself criticized the ideas of his Physiocratic friends on free trade in grain. Although he sympathized in principle with their opti-mism and their confidence that the "natural" laws of economic and social life would ensure the prosperity of all, he objected that those who had the capital resources to time their buying and selling according to market con-ditions looked like reaping enormous benefits from the free working of the laws of "nature," while the poorer farmers seemed likely to fall by the wayside. "Nature," in short, left to herself, seemed unlikely to produce a harmony acceptable to thoughtful and sensitive men.

With the marquis de Sade those doubts were deepened and gener-alized. Nature—"red in tooth and claw"—could be used, Sade argued, to justify the most appalling vice. "The motive of my dedication to evil," says one of his characters, the "chemist" Alemani, "arose, in my case, out of the profound study I have made of nature. The more I sought to discover her secrets, the more I found that she is concerned exclusively with doing harm to men. Pursue her in all her operations: you will never find her other than voracious, destructive, and malevolent  .  .  . Study her, pursue her, this atrocious nature: you will find that she never creates except to destroy, that she never achieves her ends except by murders, that, like the Minotaur, she never grows fat except on the misery and destruction of men."[51] In contrast with d'Holbach's view of nature as harmony, Sade paints a lurid picture of nature as unceasing warfare and destruction. "Murderers are part of nature, like war, plague, and famine; they are one of the means employed by nature  .  .  . So when one dares to say that a murderer sins against nature, one says something quite absurd."[52]

Against these arguments the "optimistic" materialists had in reality but feeble defenses, and if in the end their voices drowned out that of Sade, it is not because they were right or logical, but because they said what the vast majority of readers—that is, of the educated bourgeoisie— wanted to hear. In his unpublished writings Diderot faced the problem honestly. "Tout ce qui est ne peut être ni contre nature ni hors de nature," he has Dr. Bordeu say in the *Suite de l'Entretien*; "On est heureusement ou malheureusement né";[53] and the same thesis is attributed to Spinoza in the article "Liberté" in the *Encyclopédie*: "So there are no longer vicious and virtuous men? No, if you will; but there are happy or unhappy, beneficent or maleficent beings. And rewards and punishments? These words must be banished from ethics." "There is neither vice nor virtue, nothing that must be rewarded or punished."[54] In these conditions order rests not on "natural" harmony but on deterrents and other more or less violent means of repression, "Le malfaisant est un homme qu'il faut détruire et non punir." In one of his greatest works, which, significantly, he did not allow to be published, Diderot implies that the "exceptional," the "monstrous," the *individual* who is different and does not conform to the "proper" form of humanity is in fact what society is made up of. Indeed, at the end of the dialogue it is not Rameau who is an odd fellow, but the philosopher with his belief that all men are fundamentally the same and share the common notions of good and evil, beauty and ugliness.

Even d'Holbach had to confess that there are some people who cannot be educated into an "enlightened" view of their own interest, who are, in short, "assez mal constitués pour résister ou pour être insensibles aux motifs qui agissent sur tous les autres." He envisages that their actions may be "nécessaires"—that is "natural"—but in the same sentence he attributes them to the impulsions "d'une nature dépravée." Clearly the concept of nature has come under severe strain here. D'Holbach does not face the problem squarely, however. His solution is simple: "ils ne sont point propres à vivre en société." In other words, correction or elimination. But d'Holbach insists on the "morality" of this solution. Society, he argues, has a right to eliminate its recalcitrant elements. "Whatever the cause that has determined a man to act, one has a right to stop the consequences of his actions, just as the man whose fields might be washed away by a river has the right to contain its waters by a dyke or even, if he can, to alter its course. It is in virtue of this right that society, for the sake of its own preservation, may deter and punish those who might be tempted to harm it."[55] The arguments of the great demystifier have here become themselves a mystification. Who "society" is and who "*on*" is remain vague; and if the right by which society punishes those who do not obey it is founded in nature, so too, it could be objected, is the right of refusal to obey. D'Holbach can hardly conceal that the harmony of society, as he understands it and accepts it, is in reality struggle or that his own doctrine is one of "might is right." Yet he does his best to avoid facing this conclusion, as did the majority of the materialist Enlighteners.

The problems that beset the view of nature even of the materialist philosophers of the Enlightenment recur in almost all areas of Enlightenment thought. The standard doctrine of language, for instance, derived from a variety of sources including Bacon, Descartes, and Leibniz, was that language, which ought to assist our thinking, had actually corrupted it. Centuries of credulity and superstition had given birth to words that, simply because they existed, were taken to represent realities. The speculations of metaphysicians had aggravated the situation, since they consisted mostly of verbal disputes and verbal solutions. The aim of grammar in the age of philosophie and of philosophie itself must be to discover or rather to recover the philosophical language that lies below all historical languages and their encrustations of superstition, provincialism, and prejudice, and that corresponds to the fundamental structure of the human mind at all times and in all places, to those clear and distinct ideas that all men derive from their common sense experience. Philosophical grammar, in short, like nature, is a critical tool aimed at established authorities, powers, and myths.

Yet the most original of Enlightenment thinkers, without ever abandoning the ideal of philosophical grammar, began to entertain other conceptions of language. Rousseau and Diderot both saw that words have a connotative as well as a denotative function. In the *Lettre sur les aveugles* and the *Lettre sur les sourds et muets* Diderot envisages the possibility that languages are internally functioning systems whose terms acquire meaning from their relation to other terms in the system. Likewise, he began to suspect that the "discrepancy" between word and idea and between word and thing was not accidental, that it could not be done away with and that, consequently, a philosophical language which would truly represent reality or at least all men's conceptions of reality, was a chimera. All men, being absolutely unique and having unique experiences, attach different significances to different words, and even one man does not understand the same words in the same way at different moments in his life. At the limit, every man has his own language and he may even have several languages of his own. There is communication among these languages only because there is a stable element in the "system" of language. In this view, language does not reflect an objective order or a common structure of perception and thought; it is the collective repository of the thought and experience of millions who have used it and contributed to it and it passes this treasure on, as potentiality of thought and experience, to all who inherit the language. There are, in other words, no identities; individuals are neither identical with themselves nor identical with each other. Man as a fixed, stable essence is an abstraction, and so are individual persons. What is real is the collective whole of humanity, in which we all participate and which participates in all of us. The self, as Rimbaud was to say later, is another. The other is me and I am he. The object must therefore become not to find the "original" common language—that is a myth—but to break out of the limited language sphere we impose on ourselves and learn the languages of others, to open ourselves to the experience of others instead of guarding ourselves jealously from contact with them. This openness to other men, not on the assumption that they are the same underneath, philosophes below their Persians' or Indians' robes, but in full acceptance of their otherness, is the most striking and moving aspect not only of *Le Neveu de Rameau* but of that apparently typical product of philosophie, the *Lettre sur les aveugles.* Diderot's blind men do serve the standard Enlightenment function of dissolving conventional certainties, as do Montesquieu's Persians and Voltaire's Hurons and Sirians, but unlike them, they also have a life and reality of their own that the clairvoyant must *learn* to understand. The *Lettre sur les aveugles* was written, as its title proclaims not without irony, "À l'usage de ceux qui voient."

The discrepancy between words and things, as Diderot sees it, is unavoidable not only because men are not alike but because reality itself is constantly shifting and changing and is, moreover, not nicely classifiable into fixed species and genera. If reality is a constantly changing continuum, how can language, which by its very nature is discontinuous, "reflect" it? In the addition to the *Lettre sur les aveugles* Diderot speculated that music, which he understood to be continuous, might be more expressive than language, but he did not pursue this line of inquiry far.

Despite glimmerings of a view of man and language that go far beyond the ordered universe of the philosophical grammarians, Diderot never renounced the goal of philosophical grammar any more than he ever gave up the goal of a universalist morality and aesthetics based on a fundamental human nature, despite all his questioning of the concept of human nature.[56] All Diderot's most adventurous thinking ran counter to the very notion of property, enclosedness, absoluteness. If, nevertheless, he still clung to the idea of nature and to the goal of a philosophical grammar, that is, to the idea of a fundamental order of things, it is because whatever else the shifting, changing, constantly dissolving and reforming universe of Diderot might affect, property was to be preserved from it. It was not to be subject to change or question, despite some bold speculations concerning a "diablement idéal" state of affairs in which it did not exist. It was in the "nature of things" and the "nature of things" was kept in being for its sake.

Property, indeed, was the reef of which a great deal of the philosophy of the Enlightenment, and in the first instance its social philosophy, came to grief. To d'Holbach, as to Locke, property, acquired by labor, was the cornerstone of society.[57] It was to ensure property and freedom (which meant in large part freedom to acquire and enjoy property) that men bound themselves in societies in the first place.[58] "L'homme qui n'a rien dans un état ne tient par aucun lien à la société," according to d'Holbach.[59] D'Holbach's "democracy" is correspondingly a democracy of property holders, as Locke's had been. Admittedly there are great inequalities in wealth and property, but these, in d'Holbach's view, are due to fundamental physiological inequalities that enable some to work harder and acquire more than others. Though d'Holbach recognized that the acquisition of property by the strong aggravates the original differences among men by favoring those who are already favored, he still held that social and economic inequality is in the end justified by nature herself, part of the natural order.[60]

It was difficult, however, if this was so, to avoid concluding like Rousseau, that society is a jungle, and civilization repression, or to sustain the belief that the good of each is at the same time the good of all. The conflict between "society," the impersonal "one," and those men "so ill constituted as to resist or to be insensitive to the motives that determine the behavior of all the others"[61] became rather transparently a war within society between the haves and the have-nots.

Jacques Necker felt bound to admit that so it must indeed appear to the have-nots. Property, he wrote, causes grave social injustices: some men work little and profit much, others—the vast majority—eke out a bare subsistence by the sweat of their brow; some men in sickness can call upon the most skillful doctors to assist them, whereas others must share the miserable resources of charitable hospitals and workhouses; some can give their children the benefits of education, others must set them to work as soon as they are able. Property is therefore a constant source of envy, jealousy, and social conflict. It is of no avail to argue that it stimulates labor, invention, industry, and so forth. These considerations may interest the legislator but they cannot strike in the same way "l'homme jeté sur la terre, sans biens, sans ressources et sans espérances." Such a man cannot be expected to recognize the beauty of a whole "où il n'y a pour lui, que laideur, abjection et mépris."[62] It is a great illusion, Necker concludes, to hope that morality can be founded on the connection between private interest and public weal or to imagine that social laws can do without the support of religion.[63] As we mentioned before, Necker does not deny that on the basis of property society is as well-ordered as it can be. Quite simply, he says, the poor do not and cannot see that this is so. They can be brought to obey the laws only by being encouraged to believe in a harmony which they do not know in immediate experience.

The eighteenth-century materialists had projected into their view of nature their rejection of every authority that claimed to be transcendental to society itself. Insofar as their view of nature was vitalistic, putting in question all fixed categories, identities, and properties, it could be the basis of a revolutionary philosophy of love and sharing with a strong anarchist orientation, such as Diderot envisaged briefly in the *Supplément au voyage de Bougainville*. As most eighteenth-century materialists considered it, however, nature was an "objective" determining force rather than the One in which all participate and in this form it seemed to justify uncontrolled egoism and competitiveness. In fact, the revolutionary philosophy that might have flowed from Diderot's erotic conception of nature was bound to remain utopian. No social class at the time could have assumed the political program it implied.

Not surprisingly, therefore, the dominant materialist view was a mechanistic and deterministic one. Somewhat inconsistently, it is true, nature's energy was subject to two limitations. The blind working of the machine which justified individual enterprise so well was suspended where private property was concerned. The successful were *legally* insured in the enjoyment of their property on the basis of the somewhat gratuitous affirmation that property was part of the law of nature, and the forces of the state were ready, if necessary, to impose the law of nature on all who might be unnatural enough to contravene it. In addition, it was confidently proclaimed—though the evidence, as we saw, was hardly convincing—that the free-for-all of nature was actually a harmony; blind as she was, nature, after all, was declared to have a plan. Stripped of its optimistic veils, however, the materialist conception of nature was profoundly pessimistic. The reality that it mirrored back to the materialists was that of ineluctable struggle and conflict within nature, between man and nature, and between man and man. Not only was disharmony and strife the law of the empirical universe, but man himself, as part of the universe and subject to its iron necessities, must be regarded as incapable of changing anything. He could know nature, but he could not alter her; on the contrary, he had to submit to her "laws."[64]

Those who refused to bow to the nature that the philosophers of the Enlightenment had revealed, those who revolted against the world of free and unlimited competition that materialism seemed to require man to accept as necessary—and they included some of the most radical thinkers of the age—questioned the whole process by which, for centuries, men had alienated their own acts of will, choice, and repression into apparently "objective" powers or laws. To Rousseau in particular "nature" was in a way only the latest of the gods and tyrants men had created in their own image. According to him, the "natural" life of man had ended with the advent of society. Lost in the mists of myth, nature was irretrievable by social man.

The true laws of social life were not therefore to be deduced from "nature," whether the latter be viewed as the order of the physical universe or as that of the social and historical universe. From this point of view Montesquieu, the Newton of the social world, as he was frequently called, was as bad a guide as d'Holbach and the materialists. Montesquieu derived the laws of society and of social behavior not from any supposed essence of society or of man but from social phenomena themselves. Montesquieu's law, as Louis Althusser put it, "ne sera pas donnée dans l'intuition des essences, mais tirée des faits eux-mêmes."[65] Montesquieu thus dispensed with the "nature" of the rationalist tradition. But in a sense he "naturalized" the observed order of things, so that it in turn became a kind of second nature as potent as the first had been to those who believed in it. There was no place in Montesquieu's political and social typology for anything that extended beyond the bounds of the empirically observed. There was no *elsewhere* in his scheme of things, hardly a crack—reason, nature, paradise, utopia—through which novelty and change might enter an otherwise completely closed universe. Montesquieu's system has room for variety and recurrence but not for novelty. What could be observed of the past prescribed the pattern of the future and the conditions of all possible societies. It is, indeed, no secret that *L'Esprit des lois,* one of the most significant works of political science ever written, perhaps the first one in the modern sense, was also an apology of the magistracy and the aristocracy.

Against the "naturalism" of the rationalists, of the materialists, and of Montesquieu, Rousseau raised up the notion of sovereignty, of law as a means of controlling and ordering a nature that had been thoroughly transformed by social life. He thus broke with the optimism of Descartes and of a good part of the French Enlightenment tradition. Faced with the experience of the alienation of man from nature and from society, Descartes, as we saw, had tried to rationalize away the contingent facticity of things in the world and to dissolve their contradictions in harmonious geometric figures. The "real" world, nature as she "really" was, was harmony, and the rule of law was not therefore the *repression* of nature but the *expression* of nature. The pessimistic Calvinist thinkers, on the other hand—Calvin himself, Hobbes, and then Rousseau—maintained the facticity of the social and natural world and based their theories of law and sovereignty on a pessimistic world view, on the need to control and hem in or transcend a "nature" that to them, in its existing historical form, was radically different from the pure nature of the timeless world of Adam. One important strain of eighteenth-century thought is intimately bound up with this pessimistic view of nature.

In France such a view of nature seems to have been maintained primarily in milieus sympathetic to Augustinianism, notably among the Jansenists. Of course, Jansenism was concerned with the salvation of the individual Christian. The salvation of society was not one of its concerns; indeed, it was regarded as impossible. The secular radicals, on the other hand, usually thought of the salvation of the individual as dependent on the salvation of society. The modes of thought of Jansenists and of secular radicals such as Rousseau, Linguet, or even though to a lesser degree, the Utopians Mably and Morelly, had much in common, however. The concept of an "elsewhere"—utopia or absolute—played a key role in the thought of both and was the standard by which they judged an actuality from which there seemed no perspective of escape. Nor was this "elsewhere" discovered by a sleight of hand *in* the existing world, it was affirmed clearly as *opposed* to the existing world. The conflicts and contradictions of reality could not, therefore, be dispelled by Enlightenment, mere intellectual insight into and conformity with the true nature of things. They were real and could be overcome only through practical activity—whether this be conceived as revolution or as conversion.

Understandably, both the Jansenists and Rousseau, for instance, laid great emphasis on the need to change reality and to substitute another order for the existing one. Both criticized in one way or another the human habit of reading laws out of nature or history, as though these manifested an objective order which men ought to follow. The Jansenists constantly opposed their own idea of religious experience as a struggle within each man's soul between the old Adam and the new one, between nature and grace, to the post-Scholastic tradition in which conformity to natural law played a significant part in defining Christian conduct. On his side, Rousseau denounced the "nature" of the political theorists as a reification of social processes. Diderot had affirmed provocatively that everything that is, is "natural." The same line of thought led Rousseau to hold that all social life is man-made and that nothing in it is natural, not even the family, not even property—especially not property, a term that in Rousseau has an almost metaphoric power, suggestive of every kind of antagonistic shutting off of one man from another. Rousseau's own "nature," like nature before the Fall for the Augustinians, is a kind of zero point by which social (post-lapsarian) man and his institutions are defined. Similarly, the law, for Rousseau, was not outside man—in nature or in history—it was within him. Man, as Rousseau sees him, is already, before Kant, the lawmaker, and his freedom lies in living by the laws of which he himself is the conscious author. Lawmaking is thus the activity which makes him human and far from uniting him with nature, it distinguishes him from it, delimiting the two separate realms of nature and culture.

Even the contrast between the Jansenists' emphasis on practice and their social pessimism recurs in Rousseau. As Borkenau points out, Pascal could see neither a road back to feudalism nor a road forward to a new form of society.[66] The existing society, which he exposed far more thoroughly than any of his contemporaries, appeared eternal to him; consequently, he neither relativized society historically nor could he enjoin active struggle against it. Despite Rousseau's far more dynamic view of social evolution, he conceived of society as evolving in the direction of greater and greater tyranny and exploitation of the poor by the rich, the weak by the strong. With him too, therefore, an extremely radical criticism goes hand in hand with despair and in the end Rousseau turns inward, cutting himself off from society and hoping to achieve for himself the renewal he despaired of achieving for the world.[67]

Jansenism not only provided a climate in which a religious basis for radical thought was preserved, it even favored the secularization of its own radicalism. Unlike both the Protestants, who considered that every Christian had a calling in the world, and the heretical sects, for whom withdrawal from this world was the only road to salvation, the Jansenists, although they looked on the world with distaste and suspicion, neither recommended withdrawal as the only correct course of action, nor considered that everyone was bound to perform some task in it. Though some Jansenists did withdraw from the world and though the movement as a whole was closely connected with the old contemplative orders, notably the Benedictines, many others remained in the world. Others still withdrew for a spell and then returned. There was thus a constant coming and going between Jansenism and the world. The movement could not "hold" its sympathizers the way a more tightly organized sect or a religious order would have done, but it sent them back into the world with a sense of the corruption of the whole social order and, in particular, of the apparatus of the centralized absolutist state, with which they tended to identify "society."

There were, indeed, many points of contact between Jansenism and the various centers of opposition to the centralized state, both aristocratic and democratic, in the eighteenth century.[68]

Jansenism also seems to have exercised a significant influence on popular attitudes and ways of thinking, in urban areas at least, and radical modes of thought may well have been spread by parish priests before being taken over by revolutionary orators. The stronghold of eighteenth-century Jansenism was the populous parish of Saint-Médard in Paris, where, in the late 1720s, the so-called "convulsionaries" gathered around the tomb of the saintly deacon, François de Pâris. Here, among artisans and journeymen threatened by the very "progress" of the economic system that the philosophes hailed with enthusiasm, Jansenism became a popular movement, finally devolving into a form of millenarism with strong erotic overtones, and here, among these same people, the militants of the sans culotte movement emerged in the 1790s. Below the level of political theory itself, therefore, in the religious consciousness of certain sections of the French people, an ideological foundation existed on which a critique not only of existing society but of Enlightenment liberalism itself could be built.

Not all the radical critics of society emerged from the pessimistic tradition to which both strict Jansenism and Rousseau belong. Most of the Utopians remained bound in some fashion to an optimistic world view, in which nature and order were held to be identical. For Rousseau life in society was by definition unnatural: the cure for the ills of society did not lie, therefore, in a return to nature, but in a reform of the law. The good society would be achieved when the present laws, those marks of violence, by which the rich impose their authority on the poor in existing societies, are replaced by genuine laws expressing the political will of the whole people. Rousseau realized that significant economic inequality was incompatible with the state of true law, and he advocated strict control of individual wealth and property. But the restoration of equality was for him the condition of the state of law, not the condition of a "natural" society, as it seems to have been for Utopians such as Morelly (*Code de la nature,* 1755) or Mably (*Principes de morale,* 1784; *Entretiens de Phocion,* 1763; *De la Législation ou principes des lois,* 1776).

Likewise the strange Benedictine Dom Deschamps (1716–74),[69] who was in touch with some of the leading figures of the Enlightenment— Robinet, Diderot, Rousseau, as well as his patron, the marquis d'Argenson —maintained belief in a natural order of society. Deschamps had a tripartite division of history similar to Rousseau's and based, like the latter's in all probability, on a religious model: *l'état sauvage, l'état de lois* and *l'état de moeurs.* But whereas Rousseau's aim was to realize the true state of law, Deschamps's was to transcend the law altogether. Our laws are the expression of violence and domination, says Deschamps, and Rousseau would have agreed with this. But for Deschamps *all* law is constraint, even when it is self-imposed and internalized as Rousseau envisages it in the "good" society. This strange monk was as concerned with the "révolte du coeur et de l'esprit"[70] as with the revolt of the oppressed and the downtrodden politically. "By putting a brake on our most natural inclinations, our laws constantly contradict them," he wrote, "and our inclinations, being always contradicted by our laws, revolt against them and try to run their course despite them. This state of affairs necessarily brings about that condition of violence in which we are continually put in contradiction with ourselves and with each other. It is this condition of violence which makes it impossible for us to practice true social virtues to the extent that they need to be practiced, and which prevents us from living in that state of love, of peace, and of unity, that has always been enjoined upon us."[71] Rousseau too found the regime of duty (that is, of law) barely tolerable and he fled from its divisions and conflicts into dreams and fantasies of communion with nature and with others, but only the artist in him sought escape from the stern rule of the law; the moralist and political thinker remained true to the pessimistic tradition of Machiavelli, Hobbes, and Calvin. Deschamps, on the other hand, preached resolutely against *all law* in the name of man's natural freedom and a natural social order. And inevitably, we find that for him the realization of the état de moeurs in which individual desire and social order are in harmony is a matter, above all, of enlightenment, insight into the *true Système de la nature* (he had written against d'Holbach's work of that title in 1770). Hence no constraint is needed to bring the état de moeurs into being, no painful conversion, no revolution. "As evidence alone, and the clear conviction of the advantages and of the absence of disadvantages attendant upon it, are capable of giving it being, it would establish itself spontaneously, not only without bloodshed, but in peace and concord."[72]

Not surprisingly, Deschamps's optimism, with its emphasis on enlightenment, on *seeing* the "true" order of nature, ends in an appeal to the intellectuals, the cultivated and privileged classes, the enlightened despot, in short, to open the eyes of the masses and lead them into the promised land. "C'est le seul concours des hommes cultivés qui peut faire passer les hommes de l'état de lois à l'état de moeurs."[73] An "ordre des voyants" should be founded, a kind of priesthood of Enlightenment, to bring forth and preach the truth to the people. The activist theme that is so essential to radicals in the pessimistic tradition is absent from Dom Deschamps's optimistic utopianism. As there is no struggle in Deschamps against a corrupt and unruly nature, there is no need for every individual to participate in the establishment of the état de moeurs at the same level. Each member of Rousseau's state actively participates both in its founding and in its maintenance. For Deschamps, on the other hand, "it is not necessary that flocks of sheep know where to go to graze  .  .  .  ;  it is enough that the shepherds know."[74]

Both the intellectual wings of the Enlightenment, the optimists as well as the pessimists, the Catholics as well as the Protestants, worked within a framework in which law could be conceived of only as universally valid. In contrast to medieval law, which concerned itself with particular functions and privileges and which prescribed particular and concrete obligations, modern bourgeois law suffers no exceptions. But its universality was either formal, in the case of the pessimists, or ideal, in the case of the optimists. Rousseau's sovereign cannot legislate except generally. He does not concern himself with concrete cases: "L'objet des lois est toujours général  .  .  .  La loi considère les sujets en corps et les actions comme abstraites, jamais un homme comme un individu ni une action particulière."[75] On the side of the optimists, Dom Deschamps argued that in the ideal état de moeurs—man's "true" state—otherness, particularity, would simply disappear along with all class distinctions. The classless society, in short, is a prelude not, as in Marx, to the realization of individuality, but to identity. There will be only one language, Deschamps asserts, and it will be minimal, since there will be no individuality, hence no need to communicate.[76] "Les mêmes moeurs (et les mêmes moeurs ne peuvent être que les vraies moeurs) ne feraient, pour ainsi dire, des hommes et des femmes, qu'un même homme et qu'une même femme."[77]

Experienced reality, however, was more and more felt to be irreducible to universality. Correspondingly, difference was hypostatized into uniqueness. The question then arose as to what was truly real—that which was "objectively" real in reason or that which was "subjectively" real in experience. Rationality requires that the experience of difference be denied or repressed, banished inward into a realm of private fantasies incommensurate with the order of reason, shadowy, unavowable, and somehow unreal. But for many it was this realm that came to seem real and the realm of identity—the orderly, rationally understood and classified world of nature and society—that seemed unreal. Rousseau, for instance, moved back and forth between an abstract conception of men as equal and alike (at the level of society, law, and rationality) and an equally abstract conception of absolute individuality and difference (at the level of feeling and imagination) and he was never able to reconcile the two. The private, individual world of desire, imagination, feeling, and the public world of words and concepts, of moral duty and order, face each other, finally, in eighteenth-century thought in a static confrontation. Neither optimists nor pessimists could resolve the opposition between the two.

Nevertheless, it did matter whether difference was rejected as something ultimately "unreal" or as something to be conquered and repressed. Those who started out from the pessimistic, largely Protestant and Augustinian view of nature as corruption and discord, could develop practical answers to the modern problems of the scientific conquest of nature and of social order alike, but at the cost of fragmentariness and a kind of pragmatism in science—our knowledge remains knowledge of parts, not total knowledge, and it is not knowledge of reality but a convenient ordering of our experience—and of repression in morals and in politics, even if the repression was internalized to become the repression by each of his own individual (and therefore, from the point of view of society, "evil") desires. Those who started out from the optimistic view of nature as not inherently corrupt, on the other hand, a view more common perhaps in Catholic than in Protestant countries, could not maintain their optimism without idealism. But idealism provided philosophical rather than practical solutions to the problems of science and society.

In England, on the whole, the pessimistic view of nature and society remained strong. Conflict was accepted as the essence of the modern bourgeois world and men had to adjust their ways accordingly, even though in the eighteenth century there was a concerted effort to cover over this bleak picture and give what by then had become the established order the appearance of a "natural" order (Locke, Pope). In France, on the other hand, albeit with some significant exceptions, frequently among those with Protestant or Jansenist ties, the optimistic view of nature and society and the ideal of a total science of man and of nature remained very much alive. The philosophers of the bourgeoisie tried to argue that the new order was in accord with nature and that a "natural" morality was possible, that is, a way of conduct in which individual desire was in harmony with the general order.

From the beginning experience seemed to contradict this claim, so that it became necessary to argue that nature, as she truly is, lies *behind* empirically perceived nature. At this point the harmony of nature became abstract and intellectual. On the other hand, the moment the philosophes, increasingly concerned as they were with practical solutions to problems both scientific and social, turned their attention to empirical nature, their optimism became untenable. Some (Voltaire, for example) adopted the predominantly English outlook in its later, less depressing form; they thus avoided the extreme pessimism of the seventeenth-century philosophers, but their philosophical agnosticism was only a polite form of pessimism. Others (Diderot, d'Holbach, Helvétius) refused to give in and grappled bravely with the contradictions they encountered in their efforts to maintain on a concrete level the traditional optimism of the French Enlightenment, its confidence in the harmony of man and the world and in the possibility of a unified science of both. They tried not to rationalize individual desire away, as the idealists and the Utopians did; they tried instead to prove that it was, in its very concreteness, part of a total rational order. Bourgeois life, in short, was not to be accepted in its irrationality, simply because it was there; nor was its reality to be conjured away into mathematical figures. It was to be accepted in its concrete reality *because* it was rational and because any rational being must accept it. For having set themselves this task the French philosophes became in some respects the most thoroughgoing philosophers of the bourgeois world.

At the same time their very thoroughness led some of them, as they encountered more and more contradictions, to put that world in question, even while they struggled to justify it. Diderot, for instance, was mulling over or actually writing some of his most corrosive works at the very time he was laboring on the Encyclopédie. The very greatest of the philosophes were thus more than the ideologists of a class—though they were that too —for by pursuing the problems they had encountered fearlessly and with all the intellectual energy, imagination, and honesty at their command, they stretched the whole conceptual framework of contemporary thought to the breaking point and went far beyond the ideological needs of the class whose battles they had fought with skill and dedication.

## NOTES

1. There is a lucid discussion of this question by Maurice Mandelbaum, "The history of ideas, intellectual history, and the history of philosophy," *History and Theory*, 5 (1965), 33–66. See also George Kubler, *The Shape of Time: Remarks on the History of Things* (New Haven, Conn.: Yale University Press, 1962), and Siegfried Kracauer, *History: the Last Things before the Last* (New York: Oxford University Press, 1969), chapter 6.
2. The rapid growth of trade and industry in France in the eighteenth century has been discussed in Chapters 1 and 2. It has, indeed, been pointed out that the French rate of growth in this period was fairly close to that of England. Nevertheless, at least three differences should be stressed: (1) England started out from a position of higher development at the end of the seventeenth century, (2) the pattern of English production and consumption was more "advanced," the textile sector having relatively less predominance and metal goods, pottery, and so on relatively more, (3) the subsistence sector had virtually disappeared from England by the seventeenth century, having been ousted almost everywhere by the mercantile and monetary economy, whereas in France the quasi-autarchic subsistence sector was still important and acted as a brake on the growth of the economy as a whole [see F. Crouzet, "Angleterre et France au XVIIIᵉ siècle: essai d'analyse comparée de deux croissances économiques," *Annales*, 1966, reprinted in R. M. Hartwell, *The Causes of the Industrial Revolution in England* (London: Methuen & Co. Ltd., 1967), pp. 139–74].
3. Among the Marxists Engels was particularly aware of the complexity of the relations between relatively autonomous superstructures, such as law, science, philosophy, or art, and the economic infrastructure. At the beginning and the close of

*The End of Classical German Philosophy* there is a suggestion that the capacity to produce philosophies of history, at least before dialectical materialism, might be in inverse proportion to participation in the actual making of history. In the often quoted letter to Conrad Schmidt of October 27, 1890, Engels observes simply: "As a definite sphere in the division of labor the philosophy of every epoch presupposes certain definite thought material handed down to it by its pre-decessors, from which it takes its start. And that is why economically backward countries can still play first fiddle in philosophy: France in the eighteenth century as compared with England, on whose philosophy the French based themselves, and later Germany as compared with both."

4. See Franz Borkenau's brilliant and unjustly neglected work *Der Übergang vom feudalen zum bürgerlichen Weltbild* (Paris: Félix Alcan, 1934). Borkenau was one of the leading members of the celebrated Frankfurt school.

5. The relation of Calvinism and capitalism is a notoriously hot topic. Weber, Troeltsch, and Tawney, despite differences, accept that it was real. Their position has been challenged by several scholars, among them Laski in *The Rise of Liberalism: the Philosophy of a Business Civilization* (New York: Harper and Brothers, 1936) and, above all, Trevor-Roper, "Social Causes of the Great Rebellion" in his *Historical Essays* (London: Macmillan, 1957), pp. 195–205 and "The General Crisis of the Seventeenth Century" in Trevor Aston, ed., *Crisis in Europe, 1560–1660* (Garden City, N. Y.: Doubleday & Company, Inc., 1967), pp. 63–102.

6. On the relation between transcendentalism and a conception of knowledge as fragmentary, see K. A. H. Hidding, "The High God and the King as symbols of totality," in *The Sacral Kingship*, Eighth International Congress for the History of Religions, Rome, 1955 (Leiden: N. V. Boekhandel & Drukkerij voorheen E. J. Brill, 1959), especially pp. 59–60.

7. Thus Pascal's sister Gilberte writes in her *Vie de M. Pascal* that Pascal did not approve the family's interest in "des moyens pour des règlements généraux qui pourvussent à toutes les nécessités" (of the poor). "Il ne trouvait pas cela bon, et il disait que nous n'étions pas appelés au général, mais au particulier, et qu'il croyait que la manière la plus agréable à Dieu était de servir les pauvres pauvrement, c'est-à-dire, chacun selon son pouvoir, sans se remplir l'esprit de ces grands desseins qui tiennent de cette excellence dont il blâmait la recherche en toutes choses. Ce n'est pas qu'il trouvât mauvais l'établissement des hôpitaux généraux; . . . mais il disait que ces grandes entreprises étaient réservées à de certaines personnes que Dieu destinait à cela . . . mais que ce n'était pas la vocation générale de tout le monde, comme l'assistance particulière et journalière des pauvres." [*Pensées*, ed. A. Gazier (Paris: Société française d'imprimerie et de librairie, 1907), pp. 40–41.]

8. Admittedly, British philosophy appeared to become less pessimistic as the bourgeoisie acquired influence and prestige, and it could be argued that one of its main concerns, especially after the "Glorious Revolution" of 1688, was to "bury" the pessimistic and materialist Hobbes. Nevertheless, a pessimistic strain remained in British philosophy, on the whole, in its renunciation of a total metaphysic of nature and, in political thought, in a crucial ambiguity concerning the state of nature. See C. B. Macpherson, *The Political Theory of Possessive Individualism: Hobbes to Locke* (London: Oxford University Press, Clarendon Press, 1962).

9. Borkenau, *Vom feudalen zum bürgerlichen Weltbild*, p. 317.

10. 3rd Meditation, *Oeuvres*, 9, ed. Adam and Tannery (Paris: Editions du Cerf, 1897–1910), 36. (Translation mine—L. G.)

11. To Chanut, February 1, 1647, *ibid.*, 4, 608. (Translation mine—L. G.)
12. *Ibid.*, p. 610 (Translation mine—L. G.)
13. *Lettres philosophiques*, 14.
14. See Ira O. Wade, *The Clandestine Organization and Diffusion of Philosophic Ideas in France from 1700 to 1750* (Princeton, N. J.: Princeton University Press, 1938), and Paul Vernière, *Spinoza et la pensée française avant la Révolution*, 2 vols. (Paris: Presses Universitaires de France, 1954).
15. *Essay*, Book 2, Chap. 23, Para. 5.
16. *Le Philosophe ignorant*, 8.
17. *Ibid.*, 10.
18. *Essay*, Book 2, Chap. 23, Para. 12.
19. See Macpherson, *Theory of Individualism*, pp. 239–43.
20. See Emmy Allard, *Die Angriffe gegen Descartes und Malebranche im "Journal de Trévoux," 1701–1715* (Tübingen: Max Niemeyer Verlag, 1914) (Abhandlungen zur Philosophie und ihrer Geschichte, ed. B. Erdmann, Vol. 43), and Alfred R. Desautels, *Les "Mémoires de Trevoux" et le mouvement des idées au XVIIIᵉ siècle, 1701–1734* (Rome: Bibliotheca instituti historici S. J., 8, 1956). Also Werner Krauss, *Cartaud de la Villate: ein Beitrag zur Entstehung des geschichtlichen Weltbildes in der französischen Frühaufklärung*, 1 (Berlin: Akademie-Verlag G.M.B.H., 1960), 114–17.
21. First *Surprise de l'Amour*, Act I, sc. 2.
22. "Essai sur le goût," *Oeuvres*, ed. Daniel Oster (Paris: Editions du Seuil, 1964), pp. 847–48. (Translation mine—L. G.)
23. This phase is illustrated by the Calas, De La Barre, and Sirven affairs, the affair of the abbé de Prades, the proscription of the *Encyclopédie*, the burning of Helvétius's *De l'Esprit* and the attempt to reassert royal authority under Maupeou.
24. Denis Diderot, *Pensées sur l'interprétation de la nature*, 6 (Translation mine—L. G.).
25. *Ibid.*, 58.
26. *Ibid.*, 11.
27. *Ibid.*, 6.
28. The meaning of this phrase is that there is no spontaneous generation, but only the unfolding (dé-veloppement) of preexisting germs. See on this topic Jacques Roger, *Les Sciences de la vie dans la pensée française du XVIIIᵉ siècle* (Paris: Librairie Armand Colin, 1963), p. 587, fn. 16.
29. *Pensées philosophiques*, 19 (Translation mine—L. G.).
30. Fontenelle, *Oeuvres*, 9 (Paris, 1761–67), 314.
31. Voltaire, *Oeuvres*, 9, ed. Moland (Paris: Editions Garnier Frères, S.A., 1877–85), 548.
32. *Ibid.*, 27, 160.
33. *Ibid.*, 27, 220.
34. "Lettre sur les aveugles," in *Oeuvres philosophiques*, ed. Vernière (Paris: Editions Garnier Frères, S.A., 1961), pp. 119–20; "De la Suffisance de la religion naturelle," in *Oeuvres*, 1, ed. Assézat and Tourneux (Paris: Editions Garnier Frères S.A., 1875–77), 270 *et passim*.
35. *Système de la nature*, Vol. 1, Part 7, footnote, quoted by Roland Desné, *Les Matérialistes français de 1750 à 1800* (Paris: Editions Buchet Chastel, 1965), 93.
36. *Oeuvres philosophiques*, ed. Vernière, pp. 121–22 (Translation mine—L. G.).
37. *Le Vrai système, ou le mot de l'énigme métaphysique et morale*, eds. Jean Thomas and Franco Venturi (Geneva: Librairie Droz S.A., 1963), p. 187.

38. *L'Interprétation de la nature*, 2–4; article "Encyclopédie" in *Encyclopédie*; letter to Voltaire, February 19, 1758, *Correspondance*, 2, ed. G. Roth (Paris: Les Editions de Minuit, 1955–70), 38.
39. *Histoire naturelle des minéraux*, quoted by Desné, *Les Matérialistes français*, p. 130. (Translation mine—L. G.)
40. *De la Nature*, 1766, quoted by Desné, *Les Matérialistes français*, pp. 132–35. (Translation mine—L. G.)
41. *L'Interprétation de la nature*, 12.
42. *Ibid*. See Vernière's notes in his edition of the *Oeuvres philosophiques*, p. 187 and p. 258.
43. *De la Nature,* quoted by Desné, *Les Matérialistes français*, pp. 119–20. (Translation mine—L. G.)
44. *L'Interprétation de la nature*, 57. (Translation mine—L. G.)
45. *Système de la nature*, quoted by Desné, *Les Matérialistes français*, p. 122.
46. *Doutes proposés aux philosophes économistes sur l'ordre naturel et essentiel des sociétés politiques* (1768).
47. *Sur la Législation et le commerce des grains* (1775).
48. *Annales politiques, civiles et littéraires du XVIIIᵉ siècle* (1777–92), and many other works.
49. *De l'Importance des idées religieuses* (London [Paris: Hôtel de Thou], 1788), p. 33. (Translation mine—L. G.)
50. *Annales politiques*, 13, 498–99. (Translation mine—L. G.)
51. *La nouvelle Justine*, Chap. 11 (Histoire de Jérôme), in Sade, *Oeuvres complètes*, 7 (Paris: Cercle du Livre Précieux, 1962), 46. (Translation mine—L.G.)
52. Quoted by Desné, *Les Matérialistes français*, pp. 236–39. This passage could be duplicated by similar passages in all Sade's work. Perhaps the most pungent and ironical of Sade's writings is *La Philosophie dans le boudoir*, which throws a telling light on the anticlerical, Republican pamphlet "Français, encore un effort si vous voulez être républicains."
53. *Oeuvres philosophiques*, ed. Vernière, pp. 380, 364.
54. To Landois, June 29, 1756, *Correspondance*, 1, ed. Roth, 214. (Translation mine—L. G.)
55. *Système de la nature*, quoted by Desné, *Les Matérialistes français*, pp. 219–21. (Translation mine—L. G.)
56. See "Réponse à la lettre de Madame Riccoboni" (1758) in *Oeuvres*, 7, ed. Assézat and Tourneux, 403: "Dans les moeurs et dans les arts il n'y a de bien et de mal pour moi que ce qui l'est en tout temps et partout. Je veux que ma morale et mon goût soient éternels."
57. The majority of French Enlightenment thinkers shared this view of property; for a convenient synopsis of their opinions see André Lichtenberger, *Le Socialisme au XVIIIᵉ siècle* (Paris: Félix Alcan, 1895).
58. D'Holbach, *Système social*, 2, *Principes naturels de la politique* (1773), 4. See also G. V. Plekhanov, *Essays in the History of Materialism* (London: John Lane, 1934), pp. 37–51.
59. Quoted by Desné, *Les Matérialistes français*, p. 40.
60. Inequality, according to d'Holbach, "fait le soutien de la société" [*Système de la Nature*, 1, Chap. 9, 145 (Paris: Etienne Ledoux, 1821)]. D'Holbach's argument is based on a crude identification of diversity and inequality.
61. See Desné, *Les Matérialistes français*, p. 220.
62. *De l'Importance des idées religieuses* (London [Paris: Hôtel de Thou], 1788), pp. 36–37.

63. *Ibid.*, p. 40.

64. Though he placed more emphasis on education and less on physical heredity than D'Holbach, Helvétius could not see how the kind of education that he believed would transform men and society was to be realized. To change the education system, the political system had to be changed first, and how was *philosophie* to do that without first winning men over, which it could only do by a new education system?

65. Louis Althusser, *Montesquieu: la philosophie et l'histoire* (Paris: Presses Universitaires de France, 1959), pp. 26–27.

66. Borkenau, *Vom feudalen zum bürgerlichen Weltbild*, p. 488.

67. For some further suggestive comparisons of Rousseau and certain strains of Jansenist thought, see Gérard Namer, *L'Abbé Le Roy et ses amis; essai sur le jansénisme extrémiste intramondain* (Paris: Service d'Edition et de Vente des Productions de l'Education Nationale, 1964).

68. See above all the neglected study of Paul Honigsheim, *Die Staats- und Soziallehren der französischen Jansenisten im 17. Jahrhundert* (Heidelberg: Buchdruckerei von C. Pfeffer, 1914).

69. A selection of his work was published by Jean Thomas and Franco Venturi as *Le Vrai Système* (Geneva: Librairie Droz, 1963).

70. *Le Vrai Système*, p. 140.

71. *Ibid.*, p. 141. (Translation mine—L. G.)

72. *Ibid.*, p. 140. (Translation mine—L. G.)

73. *Ibid.*, p. 204.

74. *Ibid.*, pp. 204–5. (Translation mine—L. G.)

75. *Contrat social*, Book 2, chap. 6, *Ecrits politiques* (Paris: Gallimard [Bibliothèque de la Pléiade], 1964), p. 379.

76. *Le Vrai Système*, p. 119, footnote h and p. 174.

77. *Ibid.*, p. 123.

Chapter **4**

# LITERATURE
# AND
# SOCIETY

## SOME PROBLEMS OF THE
## SOCIOLOGY OF LITERATURE

The relation of literature to other aspects of culture raises similar problems to those already mentioned at the beginning of Chapter 3 in connection with the history of ideas. If anything, the problems posed by literature are even more difficult, and it would be rash to suggest that there are at present any entirely satisfactory answers. It will be most useful to outline what some of the difficulties in relating literature and society are, and what some of the directions are in which answers have been sought.

Historians may look for explicit references to events or to social types in literary works, but this is probably neither the most efficient nor the most reliable way of finding out about society. Documentary evidence is usually much better. Lesage's comedy *Turcaret,* the hero of which is sometimes taken to be the type of the financier of the late seventeenth and early eighteenth centuries, offers an example from the period we have been treating of the way in which a literary work might mislead the unwary historian. It would be imprudent to suppose that the nouveaux riches financiers were really as gross and stupid as Lesage's hero. Common sense and other historical evidence both belie such a supposition. At best we can hope to learn something of popular feelings toward financiers, though even here we should have to proceed with caution. Turcaret is so obviously a particular version of the *senex* of the New Comedy, whose traditional characteristics have simply been projected onto the convenient contemporary figure of the financier, and so much of what occurs in the play is imposed by the requirements of the genre itself, that it would be foolhardy indeed to make any direct inferences from the play to reality or from reality to the play.[1]

The plain truth seems to be that works of literature do not "reflect" social reality, at least not immediately, so that the relation between the social background and the work of literature is never a simple causal one. Literature is part of social life and a complete understanding of any society would surely include an understanding of the literature produced and consumed—to use a currently fashionable terminology—in that society, as well as of the function literature fulfilled in it. But it is possible to understand a great deal about a society without understanding or even knowing its literature. Similarly, a complete understanding of a work of literature might well include an understanding of the conditions in which it was "produced and consumed" and an insight into the role of the writer in a given society. But it is certainly possible to appreciate and to interpret a poem or even a play without an extensive knowledge of the conditions in which it was created. Some knowledge of the literary tradition and conventions that it exploits or opposes might even be more immediately useful to the literary critic than a wider knowledge of the social context. "From a methodological standpoint," the Czech critic Felix Vodička observes, "we must . . . always keep in mind that the literary work in view of the aesthetic function can be used as a historical source only with a certain caution and provided its function is duly considered, because the communication in the work in question may be subordinate to that function, especially since literary works very often have a tendency to be multivalued and to allow for various interpretations of meaning."[2]

Moreover, it is possible that literary works, like other intellectual products, are only superficially responsive to immediate social and economic conditions, and that the historian interested in determining their social significance must view history over larger periods than decades or even centuries. Big revolutions in literary history are as rare as big social revolutions. In *Le Degré zéro de la littérature* (Paris, 1953), one of the most brilliant and pregnant sketches of a sociology of literature yet written, Roland Barthes suggests that no really major literary revolution occurred in France between the Renaissance and the mid-nineteenth century. Then various social and economic changes, together with the revolutions of 1848, finally put an end to the hegemony of the classically trained bourgeoisie and the mode of writing associated with it—which the Revolution of 1789 had not altered, but confirmed—breaking down the walls of what Michel Foucault calls the *cité bourgeoise*. From that point on it was no longer possible for the bourgeoisie to ignore the reality of other classes, other values, other traditions and aspirations, contrary to its own, or to view and present its philosophy, its political theory and its writing as universal. Writers could no longer simply take a certain mode of writing for granted, following it as if it were normal in nature and reason. If they adopted it, that act was now a conscious and no longer an unconscious choice, a moral and political commitment.

A relatively successful method of linking literature and society has been proposed and exemplified by Lucien Goldmann, building on the philosophical and critical tradition of Marxism, and notably on the works of the Hungarian Georgy Lukács. Goldmann considers works of literature or art as expressions, in a given language of forms, of world views, the latter being neither individual creations—the thoughts and feelings of single individuals are too incoherent and disparate, according to Goldmann, to form the basis of a world view—nor autonomous systems, but the patterns of thought and values by which a group of men subject to common social and economic conditions tries to conceptualize and deal with its situation. Of course, there is a problem of defining what types of groups are capable of producing a world view, but that is not an aspect of Goldmann's theory that can detain us here. Suffice it to say that in Goldmann's view individual members of the group do not usually themselves realize integrally the world view of the group. It is the achievement of the writer, the philosopher, the artist, to crystallize it and give it shape, to create it in a way, since it is through him that this world view, which is seeking a form, so to speak, finds one and so comes to the consciousness of the group. It is thus the very structure or totality of the literary work that carries its true meaning and the reader should not be distracted by superficial or isolated characteristics.

The greater a work, in Goldmann's view, the more *personal* it will be, for only an exceptionally rich and powerful personality can experience or think through to the end all the implications of a view of the world that is in fact still in process of constituting itself and as yet barely defined in the consciousness of the group. But this personal quality of the work, as Goldmann understands it, is the very opposite of biographical. The more a work is the expression of a thinker or writer of genius, Goldmann holds, the more it can be understood on its own terms, without reference to the biography or the intentions of the creator. Indeed, it is the weaknesses and incoherences of a great work that have to be explained by recourse to biography and the external conditions of the life of the poet. In Goldmann's Hegelian perspective, the most powerful personality is that which best identifies with the life of the human spirit, or, in the more Marxian terms into which Goldmann himself translates this Hegelian notion, with the essential dynamics of social consciousness, in its most active and creative

aspects. To Goldmann, individual and society, in their highest forms, are
not opposed to each other. At the point at which social life reaches the
highest degree of intensity and creative energy and at which the individual
attains the peak of genius, the two become one.[3]

It is possible to see how a number of major developments in eighteenth-century literature could be approached from Goldmann's angle: the
disintegration of classical dramatic structure, for instance, into loosely
organized scenes and portraits, as evidenced in the innumerable *pièces à
tiroir* of the period from about 1670 to 1730 and even by plays such as
Regnard's *Le Légataire Universel,* which superficially retain the classical
structure of comedy; the change from the characteristic framework of
seventeenth-century comedy (the struggle of the young man with the old
man for the woman and the dethroning of the old man), which still maintains a close link to the great themes of popular culture, to the more subtle
comedy of Dufresny or Marivaux, in which the repressive "reality principle" or authority figure can no longer be revolted against, since it has
been internalized, parental figures being either altogether absent or benevo-
lent; the decline of tragedy; the passage from the picaresque form of the
novel in Lesage or even in Marivaux, with its unquestioning acceptance of
the social world that the hero explores, to the epistolary novel which
creates its own autonomous universe and, with Rousseau, a time and space,
a history and geography different from those of accepted public and social
"reality."

Nevertheless, there are objections to Goldmann's attempt to relate
literature and society and, in general, to that particular stream of the Hege-
lian-Marxist tradition of which Goldmann is only one of the latest and
more successful exponents. Indeed, his work has come under increasing
fire lately even within the Marxist camp from those who do not share his
brand of Marxist humanism and who reject what they consider its "idealist" foundations.[4] Above all, it has been objected that even in the part of
his analysis of literary works that he calls "interpretation" (the intrinsic
analysis of the structure of the work) and that he tries carefully to distinguish from "explanation" (the integrating of the literary structure into
other, "wider" structures), Goldmann does not really deal with what is
"literary" in the literary work. His study of Pascal [*Le Dieu caché,* (Paris,
1955)] has been better received, on the whole, than his admittedly more
sketchy study of Racine [first outlined at the end of *Le Dieu caché* and
subsequently given a slightly larger treatment in *Racine* (Paris, 1956)],
largely because Pascal's writing can function equally as philosophy and as
literature. Goldmann's study does, in fact, give a very revealing account
of what he calls *la pensée tragique,* but for him the literary work is simply
the incarnation of this *pensée* in words. The language of the literary work,
which to many people is the essential thing about it, seems to be for Gold-

mann simply the *means* by which ideas become manifest.[5] Goldmann has not significantly addressed himself to poetry, except for two brief and not very successful articles on Saint-John Perse.

One major objection to Goldmann's attempt to relate literature and society by way of the world view (*Weltanschauung, vision du monde*) of significant social groups is thus his inability to account for the specificity of literary expression. His method hardly distinguishes between philosophy, literature, painting, sculpture, architecture, and so on. In all these cases the "medium" of expression, if Goldmann's method is applied, can be no more than a vehicle and is in a sense accidental to the work, rather than constitutive of it. This is, indeed, a difficult position to maintain.[6]

One might also object that it is possible to "get at" the structure of literary works and to invest them with meaning in a variety of ways and that Goldmann's exclusive use of the sociological model in preference to other possible models (Freudian psychoanalytic theory, for instance, or Sartrian existentialism) as a tool to explore the coherence of the work and as a wider framework in which to integrate it and give it meaning is unwarranted. The most suitable approach may vary from work to work, and there may well be no privileged one. A text can be perceived only in a literary and ideological context, and the relation of text and context in literature resembles somewhat that of figure and ground in Gestalt psychology. But contexts vary constantly. They vary according to the life history of the individual reader who, as he rereads the "same" text, perceives it differently, and they vary according to the history of society itself, which creates new contexts for successive generations of readers. Indeed, it is the succession of contexts that permits a text to survive, and that makes it capable, within the limits set by its structure, of being infinitely regenerated. The literary text lives only as its successive "concretizations," in Roman Ingarden's term; that is, it comes to life only in so far as each reader or generation of readers invests the actual linguistic fabric with meaning. In itself the text is only a potentiality for meaning, a system of "norms," as Wellek and Warren put it in their *Theory of Literature* (New York, 1942). It is a vehicle for meanings, in other words, but does not mean in itself.

To illustrate this point, we might take the simple example of a familiar proverb—"Rolling stones gather no moss" (in French: "Pierres qui roulent n'amassent pas mousse"). The structure of the proverb with its simple oppositions—rolling/stones : no/moss—is stable, but in England and France it means that it is better not to roam so that one can dig roots and establish oneself comfortably in one place, whereas in Calvinist Scotland it means that only constant striving can save us from sinking into moldering lethargy. The same structure thus serves to organize two entirely different and even opposed meanings.

From the point of view of the sociology of literature itself, an approach such as Goldmann's is open to the objection that it turns the sociology of literature into a tool of literary analysis. (Goldmann himself would doubtless have rejected any radical distinction between the two.) Goldmann's Hegelian background leads him to be concerned almost exclusively with the *great* works, those which, as he puts it, exhibit maximum coherence and organization, and in which the human "spirit" or, in the terminology of Lukács and Goldmann, the world view of a significant social group at a significant moment in history is most fully embodied. In point of fact, maximum coherence or organic unity has not always been and need not be accepted as an evaluative criterion in literary studies. Much early literature, including folk literature, allows for a good deal of interpolation and adaptation by different artists as they produce different versions of a single basic "program." At other times, such as our own, greater value may be placed on brokenness, openness, a structure that implies self-questioning and a search for answers rather than answers themselves.

Moreover, the very category of "literature" is not something that can be taken for granted. If the performances of ancient and folk poets and storytellers, which included so many more signs than those of language alone, seem not easily encompassed by the category of literature, as we, who are primarily readers of texts, usually think of it, dramatic "literature" remains a problematic notion today. Even ideally, that is to say apart from its performance, the dramatic work makes use of a variety of signals and systems of communication over and above that of verbal language (gesture, costume, props, lighting, sound effects, and so on). What has been accepted in our tradition as "dramatic literature" is in general that which can still function when stripped down to a single set of signals (words) or that never fully exploited the resources of the theatrical medium. Students of eighteenth-century literature usually know little of the work of Lesage for the *théâtre de la foire,* for instance.

Even restricted to texts, literature has not been an entirely stable category. At the present time, many people hold that a piece of writing is literary when its primary object is not persuasion or the mere communication of information, but the verbal sign itself. During much of history, however, literature seems not to have been so narrowly and exclusively defined, and the problems that concerned critics were problems of rhetoric, rather than the question of the "essence" of literature. It is only in our time that the alienation of the literary language has become the basis of aesthetic reflection. In the classical period, history, philosophical writing, political writing, and travel reports could all be included, along with poetry, in the general category of belles-lettres. But there is no simple way of determining what will and what will not be admitted into today's more exclusive and self-conscious category of literature. Many kinds of writing can be so "framed" that they function as literature in the contemporary sense.

At the same time, many "literary" (in the modern sense) works function in society in ways that are not specifically literary. They may, like the novel in the eighteenth century to some extent, be read and valued as sources of information. They may also be thought of as disseminating ideologies, establishing or dissolving group identities, mentalities and myths, politicizing or, more frequently, depoliticizing their readers, and so on. In such cases the literary text itself, the verbal texture in which its literary quality must be sought, is or has become invisible to the reader. A study of the relations between literature and society need not, therefore, privilege the "great" work over less-organized, less-coherent works, nor need it be concerned to discover "true" meanings. It might rather be concerned with the ways in which the activity of poetry has been understood and practiced in different societies at different times.

In opposition both to the old positivist critics who often saw literary works as "reflections" of events in the world or in the author's life and to the infinitely more sophisticated critics of Hegelian, Marxist, or psychoanalytical tendency, another school of critics regards literary technique as a relatively autonomous sphere, to which content is always in a sense extrinsic. The artist, they argue, "motivates" his work by clothing it in the borrowed garb of the world of familiar experience, but the core of the work and its organizing form remain independent of the nonliterary world.

The Russian formalists of the early decades of this century were among the first to develop such views. Thus Boris Tomashevsky distinguished *plot,* the author's arrangement of a given set of materials, from *story,* the materials themselves.[7] Working with a body of literature that lends itself particularly well to formal analysis, Vladimir Propp demonstrated in his *Morphology of the Fairy Tale* (Leningrad, 1928; trans. Bloomington, 1958)—one of the major achievements of literary scholarship in this century—that it was possible to determine both the number and the order of the narrative "functions" (that is to say, those elements that advance the narrative, such as "loss," "escape," "trial," and so on) used in the Russian tales. He thus revealed that a structured program underlay the variables by which the tales were distinguished from each other, these variables being the specific realization of the functions (for example, whether the escape is effected by a magic horse or by a potion) and the selection of them. Each tale, in short, represents a specific arrangement, realized according to certain rules, of a limited number of elements, while each taletelling is the result of a collaboration between an individual artist and a tradition. Despite important differences between the folk tradition and that of written literature, Propp's work suggests that, especially in strongly codified traditions, such as folklore, popular literature, and to some extent classical literature, the meaning of a work or body of works lies not in manifest content (story), but in the arrangement and structure of fixed, formal elements.

Propp's attention was directed primarily to narrative structure itself rather than to individual stories, but many of the early formalists were more interested in the individual work fashioned by an individual artist out of familiar, traditional, and in themselves often banal materials. They set great store by technical originality, and this seemed to them a more important part of the literary quality of a work than any explicit content or "philosophy" expressed in it. Some of them became so obsessed by technique, in fact, that they made it into a decisive aesthetic value. Works in which technique is laid bare and is its own theme and object tended to be privileged over those in which technique is subordinated to other aesthetic values such as harmony or unity, and in which the highest art is the concealment of art. A method of analysis thus became itself the basis of an aesthetic.

The successors of the formalists, notably the so-called Czech structuralists—Mukařovsky, Jakobson, Wellek—have corrected this tendency. Mukařovsky distinguishes between a "structured aesthetic" and an "unstructured aesthetic." The former is strongly supported socially and it emphasizes the norm, euphony, harmony, the subordination of parts to the whole; the latter aims to infringe norms, to disrupt harmony, to reaffirm the power and energy of the individual element, usually the word, against that of the whole. At the limit, works in which the structured aesthetic predominates are banal and trivial, while those in which the unstructured predominates are unintelligible, private, and chaotic. All works of literature are situated at some point on a cord slung between these two poles, but none perfectly realizes the one aesthetic or the other, for it is only through the deviation, the unstructured, that the structure is perceptible, and it is only the structured, the norm, that makes the deviation meaningful.[8]

A somewhat similar position has been reached by the contemporary French critic Roland Barthes. According to Barthes, literature is a world that is full of meaningful signs, but that resists any conclusive statement of its meaning; that constantly invites and encourages interpretation, in other words, but that can never be definitively interpreted ("emphatiquement signifiant, mais finalement jamais signifié"). This general "anthropological" character of literature does, however, accommodate a wide range of subsidiary forms in different societies and different historical circumstances. The literary devices or *signifiants* may be strictly codified, as in classical literature, for instance, or left to seek their fortune, as in modern poetics. They can be brought close to denotation (*sens plein*) or impelled to the outermost limits of meaningfulness, where they are maximally open. But literature can never be a completely denotative system or a completely open one. It must always be suspended between the two poles of specific meaning and meaninglessness. Barthes adds that in certain periods great value may be placed on literary techniques that openly display the "deception" of literature, its artfulness, while in others the emphasis may be on clarity, simplicity, and the concealment of art.[9]

More recently still, the Soviet scholar Iurii Lotman has distinguished between what he calls an aesthetics of identity, in which the model of reality represented by the artist's work corresponds to that already held by the reader or listener, and an aesthetics of opposition, in which the model of reality represented by the artist's work is different from that of the reader, so that in the act of reading the reader is constantly striving to adjust his model to the writer's.[10]

If the early formalists seemed to rule out the possibility of a sociological approach to literature, the structuralist critics who have taken over from them have reopened this possibility at a new level. The work of Mukařovsky, Barthes, or Lotman suggests that the social significance of a literary work may lie less in its particular meanings (since it is in large measure we, the readers, who bring meaning to it) than in the aesthetic system that it exemplifies and in the relation of conformity or opposition in which it stands to that system. It seems likely, for example, that where the community is experienced as essential and the individual appears secondary or accidental, the emphasis in poetic theory and practice may well be on clarity, the observation of established conventions, and the fundamental likeness or universality of things, and that where the individual is experienced as concrete, while the community and its values appear abstract, the emphasis will be on openness of meaning, on poetic invention, and on the creation of novel and unexpected relations of likeness whose purpose is to subvert the old ones.

## WRITING AND WRITERS IN EIGHTEENTH-CENTURY FRANCE

Eighteenth-century literature appears to stand somewhere between the two aesthetics described by Lotman. In many respects it is oppositional, rejecting existing stereotypes of reality and searching for new models. Diderot's novel *Jacques le fataliste* and his writings on and experiments in the theatre (his plays, I believe, are best regarded as experiments designed to serve as a basis for theoretical discussions) are doubtless extreme forms of this tendency in eighteenth-century literature, but they are not isolated cases. The eighteenth-century writer tried out many new forms of literary expression. At the same time, however, he accepted, on the whole, the literary language he inherited from his predecessors and was not even particularly aware of it as "literary." It was simply the language people used when they wrote—be it history, essays, letters, or novels. Even in its opposition, in short, eighteenth-century literature enjoyed the luxury and security of being able to take its language for granted as normal, not alienated from everyday life and speech, but integrated into them. Characteristically, the eighteenth-century writer did not, on the whole, feel alienated from his public, nor did he think of literature as something radically distinct from history or philosophy or even political theory. Literature was not yet a problem to itself.

In another domain, this security can be observed in the plates illustrating Montgolfière's amazing balloons or in the plates of scientific instruments published with the *Encyclopédie*. These continue to follow neoclassical principles of composition and design. Similarly, the accounts of travelers returning from voyages to Africa or the Pacific rarely lose that faintly ironical decorum that is so characteristic of the eighteenth century, and the illustrations confirm the appropriation of the alien by the familiar. The irremediably other in the eighteenth century was simply not recognized: it could be neither understood nor talked about. The *cité bourgeoise* was still impregnable. Even Diderot's Tahitian was schooled in French rhetoric.

Opposition usually meant, in fact, going back to an earlier and purer model. The "original genius" in the eighteenth century should probably be thought of less as a man able to produce something original (in the sense of new) than as a man who has access to the original (in the sense of first) models of things and of man himself—to man and nature, in short, as they were before the incrustations of social convention. Literature and art are thus still conceived of as imitative rather than inventive or productive activities. The oppositional model of the eighteenth-century writer, in other words, is not usually presented as historically new, a projection into the future, but rather as the image of a universal original, which the prejudices that have come with historical development prevent us from seeing. Bourgeois aesthetics, like bourgeois political theory, did not see itself as bourgeois or justify itself historically. It saw itself as universal, reflecting the very essence of man.[11]

Eighteenth-century literature manifests its ambiguous character— oppositional, yet in large measure also traditional—at the ideological level also. Critical of established ideas and practices as it was, it was also further, perhaps, than literature had been since the Middle Ages from that popular culture of which it had once been part. In the "philosophy" of the folk, which continued to find expression in the antics of jesters and tumblers and in the pantomimes and vaudevilles of the *théâtres de la foire,* everything that claims to be eternal, fixed, separate, is negated, while, on the contrary, the complementarity of all things in the world, their perpetual changing and becoming, and the necessary relatedness of birth and death are affirmed.[12] As Lanson suggested seventy years ago, a good deal of this old outlook survives in Molière at a deeper level perhaps than the social comedy with which he skilfully interwove it;[13] it is almost completely gone from the work of Destouches or Nivelle de la Chaussée. At the same time, however, eighteenth-century literature and thought did occasionally renew itself at this very source.

But by the eighteenth century the source itself was muddy. The idea of universal communication, of eros as ruler of the world, of knowledge by feeling rather than seeing, of continuity rather than discontinuity as the principle of the universe survived modern modes of thought not only in the "philosophy" of the folk but in elitist and hermetic doctrines inherited from the Renaissance. The two strands appear frequently to have come together, as in the strange and still little understood phenomenon of the "Jansenist" convulsionaries or shakers of the 1720s or in the amazing Mesmerist craze that swept France in the last decades of the century.[14]

In Rousseau's *La Nouvelle Héloïse* this ambivalent undercurrent of resistance to modern rationalism—itself part of the movement of Enlightenment—encountered the dominant, rationalist strand of Enlightenment thought, and in the encounter the Enlightenment discovered some of its own internal contradictions. The novel is virtually split into two parts. The first celebrates the revolt of eros against authority, of the son (Saint-Preux) against the father (the baron d'Etange) and the connivance of the woman (Julie and, somewhat ambiguously, Madame d'Etange) with the son; the second part marks the submission of eros to reason and authority, of the son (Saint-Preux) to the father (Wolmar) and the latter's recapture and taming of the woman. The revolt itself remains ambiguous, however, because the prerational world offers no unified opposition to the authority of reason. The love of Julie and Saint-Preux can be interpreted both as an affirmation of the rights of the body and of the instinctive life, with strong popular and democratic overtones, and as a longing for a utopia of "belles âmes" in which escape can be sought from the everyday world with its institutionalized relations of authority and subordination. The two meanings are deeply entwined in the novel as they may well have been in the thinking of many eighteenth-century men and women.

One of the most popular of eighteenth-century novels, Prévost's *Manon Lescaut,* had already foreshadowed some of the principal themes and patterns of Rousseau's novel. Both the social and the erotic meanings are as ambiguous in Manon as they are in *La Nouvelle Héloïse.* Lacking any stable identity, reflecting only the desires and evaluations of others, playing many roles, an undecipherable enigma to her lover—who, incidentally, betrays many of the characteristics he deplores in his mistress and functions with respect to certain other characters in the novel (Tiberge, the father superior of Saint-Lazare) much as she functions with respect to him—Manon is the very incarnation of Regency worldliness, of a universe without fixed essences or ultimate values. Yet at the same time as her Parisian existence is implicitly condemned—Manon becomes her "true" self only in the "natural" world of Louisiana—it is painted in extremely attractive colors. And in the end, the age-old figure of the prostitute, the worldly, corrupt woman who has lost her "identity" evokes as in a distant echo the mythical figure of Eros, the great force that subverts every order and denies every essence.[15] In a contemporary disguise eroticism masks Eros and the sex object figures the great mother. This mythical dimension of Manon emerges most powerfully in the scene where, after an allusion to *le parfait amour* that inevitably recalls the doctrines of courtly love, des Grieux buries his mistress "au sein de la terre," thus returning to earth "ce qu'elle avait porté de plus parfait." The pathos of this scene is hard to acccount for, unless we can allow that the mythical theme has subterraneously accompanied the contemporary social one all along, undermining from within the support the novel apparently gives to ideologies of authority and identity and its almost Jansenist condemnation of "distraction." The story of Manon is after all a series of encounters between the son and the father or various father figures, in which the former tries to wrest the woman from the latter and hold her for himself. From the beginning, the rivalry of son and father is expressed in the humiliating taunts des Grieux's father addresses to the young hero after Manon's first abandonment of him; but it is when des Grieux compares his own love for Manon with his father's love for his mother that the masks fall and the rivalry is most clearly exposed. "Ne me parle plus de ta mère," the father exclaims in rage.

As des Grieux's search for values in a valueless world takes place in a degraded way, so Manon represents a degraded, tarnished image of Eros. The degradation cannot, however, completely conceal the nature of the elements at play in this strange novel. And the power and significance of the work, as well as its relevance to the Orphic theme of the poet as the emissary of the underworld, become more apparent when we recall that des Grieux is the narrator of his own tale, the figure of the poet himself within the tale. The poet is recalling in fact his age-old relation to eros, to the underworld of passion and energy that the social order has repressed. But he does it, as one might expect, in an ambiguous way because his own relation to this underworld is ambiguous. It is both that which calls and that from which there must be protection. Manon is both the object of desire, comforting, maternal, the great One in which all wounds and separations are healed, and the devouring abyss that destroys all identity and individuation, the white goddess and the black. In the end, order is restored as Manon goes back down into that underworld from which she came, leaving in the reader's mind, as in des Grieux's, the disturbing memory of a turbulent force that might at any time erupt again to turn the world upside down. The author has done his duty. He has invoked the monster, but he has repudiated and transfigured her, thus reaffirming the established order of things. The preface, like the prefaces to *La Nouvelle Héloïse,* reveals the same ambiguity. The tale is told, we are informed in good Aristotelian fashion, in order to lend support to morality and orderly behavior by purging the passions and warning of the dangers that lie in wait for the unwary and the innocent.

By recalling, however timidly or circumspectly, aspects of life and of reality, or ways of conceiving them, that were ignored or suppressed by official ideologies, institutions, and languages, eighteenth-century literature became not a reflection but a contestation of official reality. Likewise, eighteenth-century writers began to question and to break down the strict codification of the genres and even that of the different arts themselves, which classicism had labored so hard to institute. New forms of expression were tried out (the *mélodrame,* for instance, in Rousseau's *Pygmalion,* or the *journal intime* in his *Rêveries*) and existing forms were renewed or altered (the dialogue, the novel). The question of the relation between art and life itself was brought to the fore again and examined, notably in the work of Rousseau and Diderot, and the reassuring frontier dividing them laid open to review. When the eighteenth-century writer appeals— as writers often do in periods of aesthetic uncertainty—to "sources" or "objective evidence" in order to bolster the "reality" of his fiction, what are we to make of his claim? Is he, with more or less conscious shrewdness, trying to reassure the timorous or the suspicious that his work is no dangerous artistic fantasy, but a faithful copy of reality? Doubtless that is one of his aims. But what is, in fact, the "reality" he is "copying"? Frequently it is one that the reader has not noticed, has forgotten, or has suppressed, and the writer's revelation of it is in fact a contestation of official reality.[16] Moreover, the writer can probably count on his more sophisticated readers not to forget that the world into which the author has taken them is an imaginary and fictitious one and to recognize that the appeal to reality is a literary device, itself part of the structure of the work, which raises rather than resolves the question of the relation of works of imagination to reality. The effect of the appeal to reality is, in fact, double-edged. The fictitious is made to seem real and the real may appear to be fictitious. The reader may be led to ask whether such things really happen. Is reality perhaps less cozy and sure than it seems? Can we take for granted that we know what it is, that fiction and reality, the imaginary and the real are two clearly separated spheres? Is the whole of reality embraced by officially institutionalized categories of thought and language, or does not fiction reveal as part of reality a disturbing potential in man himself that both traditional authorities and our own desire for security lead us to ignore or repress?

Few eighteenth-century writers of fiction made these questions explicit in their works. Most frequently the author played a game of hide-and-seek, sometimes raising questions, sometimes pretending, or even—to the degree that he had internalized his society's judgment of the artist as dangerous and sought to stifle his own questioning—believing that his fictions raised no problems and disturbed no established canons, but merely repeated the real. On the other hand, a bold writer such as Diderot made of the problematic relation of fiction and reality the very theme of his novel *Jacques le fataliste*.[17]

Roland Barthes has shown how in the plates of the *Encyclopédie* an ordinary, easily recognizable view of everyday objects, such as coaches, shops, implements of one kind or another, animals, parts of the body, explodes into an almost surrealist fantasy world in the lower part of the plates, where the everyday objects are analyzed and their components parts magnified, distinguished, and portrayed with great "realism."[18] In a similar way, the literary appropriates wider and wider spheres of reality in the eighteenth century as it becomes "realistic," but at the same time it also invades reality, defamiliarizing it and injecting into the most ordinary, everyday occurrences and phenomena the poison of doubt, uncertainty, and possibility.

Nevertheless, though it proclaimed its emancipation from the past and its rejection of old myths, though it questioned much that was taken for granted, eighteenth-century literature did not, as a rule, attack fundamental and reassuring assumptions about the permanence or reality of certain universals, such as nature or reason. Modernism did not yet carry in itself the worm of solipsism, and communication was not yet a severe problem for the writer. Society, relations with others, a common humanity grounded in nature and reason, and above all a common language, still seemed in the main to be concrete realities, and they were taken for granted, even as particular social arrangements, institutions, and beliefs were demystified and exposed as absurd, grounded in nothing. Eighteenth-century writers, as a group, thus had more in common with each other and with their public, and even with tradition, than their nineteenth- and twentieth-century successors.

Their literary practice does, however, reveal some differences among them concerning the nature of literature and of culture in general. These, in turn, imply different views of man and society, which, though not radical, may be politically and socially significant. It may be worth exploring briefly these conceptions of literature and culture in the work of the three best-known French writers of the century.

Of the three—Voltaire, Diderot, and Rousseau—the one who most readily accepted that literature (by which we mean the so-called high literature, folk culture being always another matter altogether) constituted an autonomous realm, separate from truth, or nature, or original being, was Voltaire. For Voltaire, literature, like culture in general, was still the product of a group rather than of individuals, but it was the product of an elite group, which was as sharply distinguished in Voltaire's mind from the mass of humanity as literature itself was distinguished from folk poetry or culture. Voltaire's work almost always suggests that the realm of literature and of civilization as a whole is an autonomous and artificial one— an island, a garden, a Cirey or a Ferney—which a relatively small group of men carve out for themselves at certain favorable moments in history and in which alone freedom and humanity are realized. Civilization, indeed, as Voltaire sees it, might be defined as the construction and elaboration of human systems of meaning. Natural (in the sense of original) man and natural (in the sense of original) art or language are not privileged in Voltaire's thinking. On the contrary, they are associated with the rude, the uncouth, the popular—that which men must in fact transcend in order to realize their human nature. In other words, Voltaire was not a self-conscious champion of the *unnatural.* He simply did not identify human nature with an original model but saw it rather as a form that could be and was realized throughout history only by a few. The fullest realization of humanity and civilization is thus bound up, in Voltaire's view, with a kind of aestheticizing of all aspects of life, until all transcendental meanings and all meanings not clearly made and assumed by men themselves have been demystified and removed. Eating, clothing, talking, sexual activity, every form of social living, must strive to be a self-contained system, so to speak, referring to itself and to nothing beyond itself, independent both of nature (in the form of physical need) and of reference to supposedly objective historical or religious realities. Voltaire did what he could to transform even his notorious hypochondria—the unconscious and unwilled sign of his horror of nature—into a role chosen and shaped by himself. Correspondingly, literature, as he saw it, must seek to extend its domain over all language, progressively reducing the scope of language both as a means of instruction—in which sense it is not different from animal languages—and as a supposedly transparent reflection of reality, bearing meanings commanded not by itself but by that reality. It cannot even simply exist alongside reality, obediently elaborating recognized literary themes in recognized ways. It must go out and invade as much of the domain we call reality as possible.

At the same time, however, Voltaire does accept that there is a reality beyond all our highly contrived human systems, an impregnable, undecipherable otherness that can only be repressed or concealed, not eliminated, and that may irrupt unaccountably into the human order in the form of earthquakes, wars, popular "fanaticisms," illness, and death (all of which Voltaire places in the same category). Thus the rococo salon, though it is an autonomous universe of purely human signs, does not destroy or supplant the wood, stone, and lead from which it is made; the most exquisite meal—and Voltaire has a penchant for culinary description—is still concocted from dead animals and fish; and the most self-contained and self-conscious work of literature uses a linguistic material that also serves mundane, practical, and purely instructional purposes. Like all the arts of civilization, literature, for Voltaire, is a kind of cosmetic, skillfully working over and building its own system out of an irrational and basically unintelligible material which it can never overcome and on which in the last resort it is dependent. For it is from this inhuman, alien element, from these repulsive "origins," that men emerge, just as they vanish back into them—"petits papillons d'un moment" as Voltaire himself put it in his poem *Adieux à la vie*—at the end of their brief careers.

The political and social significance of this conception of literature is not easily established. It might be argued that it gave an objective and "universal" form to the situation of a highly intelligent, sophisticated, and articulate society, which had demystified its own repressive social and historical institutions but was unable to renounce them and become truly revolutionary. Thus Voltaire could see no bridge between reason and historical reality, no way of intervening in the processes of history; the latter appeared as objective, uncontrollable and fundamentally inhuman as nature herself. The only revolutionary act that could be accomplished was the constant unmasking of every rationalization of history and of social reality in general. More broadly, however, Voltaire's view of literature and culture might be interpreted as characteristic of the age of bourgeois cultural hegemony, which he himself contributed to. The immutability of the fundamental literary values through the ages, their primacy with respect to all other arts and activities (culture, for Voltaire, is primarily literary, the culture of the book), their opposition to virtually every form of popular expression, and indeed the need to preserve them from this destructive force—these positions may well seem intimately linked to the values and the general ideology of the bourgeoisie.

Voltaire's view of literature, which was close to that of many other writers in the eighteenth century (Fontenelle, for instance, despite some disagreements on detail) and which has enjoyed a long life since, was not shared by Diderot or Rousseau, neither of whom accepted Voltaire's peculiar version of dualism—that is to say, the admission that there is an ultimate reality and at the same time the shutting out, so to speak, of that reality. Diderot recognized that literature was not a reflection either of *la belle nature* (the orderly universe supposedly underlying the chaos of particular experiences, the *vraisemblable* as opposed to the *vrai*) or of a supposedly immediately perceived reality. In fact, he questioned whether any perceptions are immediate. But he still conceived of literature as standing in a fruitful relation to reality and to nature. (In an analogous way he utilized for his own works elements taken from the various forms in which popular culture still survived in his time. Diderot's work is complex and sophisticated, but it maintains a living link with the traditions of French popular culture. This is particularly striking in *Le Neveu de Rameau*.) The aesthetic, for Diderot, is not distinct from other aspects of human life. It is related both to the erotic life and to the activity of the intellect. Indeed, it is an essential moment in the expansion of the conceptual categories by which men try to grasp the inner forms and processes of nature. There is thus no fundamental opposition between nature and culture, as there is no opposition between body and mind. Both are part of and generative of a constantly changing totality, which is the real. Nothing, in Diderot's world, is absolutely separate from anything else. Everyone is at once an individual and a participant in other individuals. The self is inhabited by the other and the other inhabits the self. Civilization itself can only be conceived as a *collective* enterprise. In a similar way, the aesthetic, the intellectual or rational, and the erotic are intimately connected, even though they are also distinct. The enrichment of human culture for Diderot seems to result from the constant creation of different experiences and different perspectives through specialization and individuation (of persons, peoples, classes, disciplines) and from the enlargement of the understanding that comes from the reintegration of these varied experiences and perspectives.

For Rousseau, language and literature were neither Voltaire's autonomous realm of convention nor, as they were for Diderot, a means by which a richly varied humanity stores and extends its categories of understanding. Rousseau conceived of his search for reality as a return to origins, the recovery of a lost original self and of a lost relation to nature. The intensity of his experience of alienation seems to have led him more and more to think of nature in a rather abstract way, almost as a kind of general metaphysical being in contrast to the equally abstract generalized evil, which society came to represent for him. Similarly the self and the other became so polarized in his thinking, that the relation between them—and here we touch on a fundamental difference between Diderot and Rousseau —could be conceived only as total separation, opposition, and hostility, or as total identity and fusion. As he tried to exorcise from his person all the accretions of social and cultural experience and to discover at the end of this unique experiment the original Adam that social man is too corrupt even to remember (his famous quarrel with Diderot is surely part of that refusal to admit any indwelling of others in himself) he came increasingly to dream of a new language to express that original self and its intuitions. For existing language, the product of culture, would be totally incapable of conveying them. The search for an original pure self brought Rousseau closer and closer to the loss of self; similarly the search for an original pure language led him progressively closer to the edge of silence. At the end of his career, in the second of the *Rêveries d'un promeneur solitaire,* Rousseau recounts a remarkable episode in which, after being knocked down accidentally by a Great Dane, he awakens to what he presents as an immediate awareness of or presence to Being. But no language can tell this experience, and Rousseau, writing it up after it happened, can hope at best to suggest it obliquely. In the course of his career Rousseau thus came ever closer to making literature out of the impossibility of literature as he dreamed of it. Unable to create the new language he wanted, to say the only thing worth saying—yet unsayable— he found that the more he wrote in order to tell the truth directly, to turn the inside out, as it were, the more his writing became a demonstration of the impossibility of telling it directly.

The increasingly fragmentary character of Rousseau's work bears witness to his persistent effort to escape from routines of language, narration, and presentation and to make his language a means of discovering the true self rather than a means of covering it. But Rousseau never claims to have succeeded. His work comes closer to poetry than much eighteenth-century writing, but it remains on this side of prophecy. Moreover, a large part of his work—notably his novel *La Nouvelle Héloïse* and his *Confessions*—owes its existence to his exploitation of less-refined materials than the experiences described in the second or even in the fifth *Rêverie*. (The latter contains the episode in which Rousseau describes his strange state of consciousness as he lay in a boat on the lac de Bienne). From immediate presence to Being there is, after all, almost invariably a more or less rapid falling away in which the disaster of the first Fall is repeated. Besides, such states of grace are at best intermittent. They cannot, or could not then, be induced, and they may never recur or even occur. The *rêverie* of the lac de Bienne is more easily induced, but it too represents a relatively rare, privileged experience. Such isolated episodes took Rousseau to new pinnacles as a writer, but they also brought the paradox of literature to an uncomfortable head. For the main body of his imaginative writing prior to the *Rêveries* and even for the majority of these, Rousseau relied on a different kind of material, coarser perhaps, but more serviceable,—memories of past experiences and fantasies or reflections connected with the everyday world. From them he forged a relatively durable refuge from and alternative to the misery of his alienated historical existence, a more habitable and even a more satisfying utopia than that offered by the Adamitic intuition of the second Rêverie or the half sleep of the fifth. The experiences described in these two Rêveries represent an overcoming of the opposition of self and other by denial of one of the terms of the opposition (the self in the case of the second Rêverie, the other in the case of the fifth). In writing of them, however, and thus in a sense "betraying" them, Rousseau restored the term that had been eliminated.

In general, literature seems to have been for Rousseau a means of reconciling what civilization had sundered: objectivity and subjectivity, historicity (the fall into time) and essence. Through its transformation into literature, reality was freed from history; it ceased to be the oppressive other and became subject, to some extent, to the author's control. In many respects literature was the closest thing Rousseau could find to that miraculous second stage of nature, "la véritable jeunesse du monde," which is glowingly recreated in the *Second Discourse*. In the second stage of nature—as, subsequently, in the Greece of Schiller and Goethe—individuality and subjectivity exist, but they are not yet defined by their opposition to and exclusion of the other. There is a kind of porousness of things and persons at this stage that permits opacity and therefore individuality while maintaining a degree of transparency, that is of oneness, undifferentiation. *Community* is, indeed, this middle state—neither oneness nor separateness, neither undifferentiation nor complete differentiation. Literature, to be sure, is absent from this happy world of Rousseau's historical imagination—only song and dance are known to it—for literature, especially *written* literature, separated from gesture and the singing voice, arises only when differentiation has set man against nature, others, and himself. Literature is the very token, for Rousseau, of that fatal Fall whose lamentable consequences are recounted in the Second Discourse. As such, Rousseau constantly rejected and condemned it. On the other hand, only in literature could he find even an illusory healing of the wounds suffered by modern man and modern society. Toward the end of the fifth Rêverie he suggests the importance for his literary enterprise of absence: things and people appear to him more vividly, he claims, in recollection or literary recreation than they ever did when physically present. The reason for this is that in the literary work absence and presence, transparency and opacity, self and other, subject and object, dream and reality, fiction and truth— everything that civilization, in Rousseau's analysis, has split into antagonistic opposites—can seem to merge into one another. Referring beyond itself to a world outside, yet at the same time preserving its autonomy, literature embodies the transcendence of these unfortunately created opposites. For this reason it becomes, for Rousseau, a utopia, an indictment of present social reality and a consoling substitute for the lost Paradise.[19] A great deal of his work is dedicated to the retrieving of reality through writing. The very last piece he wrote—the moving tenth Rêverie that opens

"Aujourd'hui, jour de Pâques fleuries, il y a précisément cinquante ans de ma première connaissance avec Madame de Warens"—is a final re-creation in literature of a crucial part of his life to which he constantly returned in an effort to grasp it as he could not grasp it at the time he lived it.

At the same time as Rousseau pursued literature, however, he denounced it, for the reasons we have already suggested. If it was a hint of Paradise, literature was also the sign of that cleavage which marks the Fall and which makes its consolations necessary. Significantly, Rousseau accepts in anticipation the judgment of literature by a rationalized bourgeois society. He justifies it only halfheartedly as a personal consolation, valid for himself alone; it is not recommended for the many, and it is associated with *dolce far niente,* innocent idleness, and dreams. Literature, for Rousseau, is at once a revolt of the imagination and a mutilation of it, a reassertion of freedom and wholeness against the grim ethics of a repressive and alienating society and, at the same time, an acceptance of defeat.

Rousseau's conception of literature and his experience of the literary venture, so unlike both Voltaire's and Diderot's, manifests his modernity more intensely than any specific content of his work. For Voltaire and Diderot alike—and to us they must seem to have lived in an almost paradisiac world—the group for whom the writer wrote, the world to which he addressed himself and that came to consciousness of itself through him was still a concrete one. Voltaire's was remarkably broad but intensely concrete at its relatively large center. (Voltaire was in personal contact, either directly or through his close friends and representatives, with a vast number of people, who were his immediate audience.) Diderot's was broader and already more ideal, since it transcended, in the author's own image of it, the historical present. Diderot's very attempt to broaden the base of his work, and to unite in it high and low culture, the philosopher and the tramp, the scientist and the visionary or poet, meant that he could not fully conceive his readership (the community that spoke through him and discovered itself in his words), since it had in fact already been radically split, the bourgeois and the aristocracy being much further from the people than at any time in the history of France. Diderot thus had to project a posterity that would value his work, on the one hand, and, on the other, to restrict the concrete public of his most original works to a very small number of intimates. Neither Diderot nor Voltaire, however, experienced the acute alienation of Rousseau or suffered with him the exile of the poet and the mutilation of the whole human being, and it is through these experiences, above all, that Rousseau heralds the age to come.

In some respects, as Sartre suggests in *Qu'est-ce que la littérature?,* the eighteenth century attained a happy equilibrium between writer and public. The former had not yet paid for his freedom by becoming alienated and the latter, although it was increasingly dominated by the bourgeoisie and was already beginning to be exploited in a capitalist way, was neither monolithically tyrannous nor anonymous and abstract. Moreover, writers and public subscribed in large measure to a common, predominantly bourgeois set of values. The disintegration of the reading public into a series of self-contained publics, each with its own demands, its own suppliers, and virtually its own language, had not yet occurred. True, as Robert Mandrou recalled recently, the vast majority of French people in the age of Enlightenment did not participate much in the "higher" culture that we have incorporated into our literary and philosophical tradition and that we study in our schools and colleges.[20] The gulf between high and low culture was, if anything, wider than it had ever been. At the same time, however, because of the general rise in prosperity and various changes in the book trade that accompanied it, the higher culture was accessible to wider social groups than it had been. It thus drew more and more talent toward itself, impoverishing the popular culture, which became in effect less and less popular, more and more simply low, and more and more invisible. Indeed popular culture was already on the way to being in some measure an ersatz created *for* the people by writers who were in no sense *of* it but sought instead, albeit still only half consciously, to manipulate it. There is no Villon and no Rabelais in the century of the democratic revolution. In short, the bourgeoisie had virtually monopolized literature.

At the same time, the character of the high culture was itself slowly changing under the impact of its own success. Even in the seventeenth century, many readers were also writers, and Racine and Boileau paid serious attention to the judgment of the public. By the eighteenth century high culture itself was beginning to be produced for a public of which a considerable part was not culturally sophisticated, though it aspired to be. In short, there were signs that high culture might become as much a market operation as low culture and that the relation of writer and public might come under a new kind of strain. Thus in Diderot's *Jacques le fataliste* the relation of author and reader is an aspect of the central theme of the relation of servant and master. The impatient reader (the master) who wants to call the tune—and characteristically it is a familiar stereotyped tune— is constantly reminded by the narrator (the Jacques) that he possesses only the shadow of authority, not its substance, and that he may lose it at any time. The narrator, moreover, with a great deal of teasing, insists on telling his story "as it happened," that is, in a way that does not necessarily conform to the master's wishes and expectations. The author's purpose, in sum, is not simply to pander to the public's desire for reassuring routines, but to shake it up and change it.

In a valuable study of the French book trade in the Old Regime,[21] David Pottinger has shown that between the sixteenth and the eighteenth centuries the large folio and quarto volumes of the Humanist age became progressively more rare. In the eighteenth century the percentage of pocket-sized duodecimos rose phenomenally. It was, indeed, the age of the *portatif,* and many works carried this word in their title. Although we cannot compare this development with today's paperback revolution, the sheer magnitude of which renders it qualitatively different, it can be taken as a sign of the spread of high culture among larger segments of the population and of a considerable growth of the reading public. Admittedly, we have little information on the volume of books produced in the eighteenth century. We know that *La Nouvelle Héloïse,* for instance, went through at least fifty editions (not counting pirated editions, of which there must have been many in view of the popularity and success of the work) in the period between 1761 and 1800, but we have no way yet of determining how many copies were actually printed and published.[22] We know very little about the size of editions. Nevertheless, there is other evidence of a very considerable increase, in the eighteenth century, both in the number of works published and in the number of books actually produced and circulated.[23]

The increasing specialization of the book trade and its greater need of capital are in themselves signs of the expansion of the market. Renaissance printers had been publishers, booksellers, and even authors or editors too. In the eighteenth century all these functions were separated: printing, production, wholesale and retail distribution were more and more handled by different persons or companies. The capital required for some publishing enterprises was so great that several publishers had to band together. The *Encyclopédie,* for instance, was financed and launched by such a syndicate, and it was to the pressure these businessmen were able to bring to bear on the government that Diderot owed his release from the prison of Vincennes in November, 1749. Press magnates such as Charles Panckoucke began to emerge—men who held control of a variety of publishing enterprises. In general, publishing gradually ceased to be a craft exercised in close relation with its clientele and became part of the growing world of capitalist business. The great Kehl edition of Voltaire, for instance, was not simply a work of piety; it was a business venture from which Beaumarchais, an indefatigable speculator as well as a writer, hoped to make a handsome profit. The growing number of reviews and periodicals also points to an expansion of the market.

As the market grew and its character changed, as it became more bourgeois, the type of literature that was produced for it began to alter. Pottinger and others have shown that between the sixteenth and the eighteenth centuries there was a shift in what people read. The proportion of books on theological subjects, for example, declined constantly during the whole period. By the 1780s such works represented only 2 percent of works published with *permission tacite* (semiofficial permission)—an understandably low figure, since most theological works would qualify easily for full official *approbation*. Even in this latter category, however, theological works came lowest in the scale. On the other hand, works of literature, history, political theory, science, economics, as well as practical manuals of all kinds increased steadily in number until, on the eve of the Revolution, they made up all but a fraction of the total production of the book trade.[24]

Newer genres, the essay, the *drame,* the novel, were more important in fact if not in theory. The vogue of the novel was particularly marked, reflecting a change not only in taste, but in reading habits and in the reading public. The novel is a private and bourgeois, not a public and popular genre. It is intended to be read, not spoken or heard (it thus supposes not only privacy but literacy) and to be enjoyed at each reader's own pace, in his own time, and in the place he selects. Moreover, in its eighteenth-century form it participates to some extent in the bourgeois, scientific culture of the Enlightenment. Rather than a unified poetic work whose meaning and relevance is inseparable from its literary quality, the novel could be thought of as a lesson. From this point of view, the imaginative part of it was secondary, mere diversion; the serious part of it lay in the information it provided. In an increasingly fragmented, yet at the same time increasingly encompassing society, novels became instruments of knowledge and power, guides to success, means by which individuals in closed social groups or communities could open their horizons and find out about the world. The novel is in a way a semidocumentary genre in the eighteenth century and its close relation to travel literature is not, probably, fortuitous. It was almost surreptitiously that the artistic function became the dominant one in it. To the contemporary reader, moreover, the communicative function was probably always important.

Thanks to the expansion of the market, the eighteenth-century writer was freed from academicism, which had meant fairly strict control of literature by the government and a homogeneous ruling elite. The decline of the court, the shift of the artistic center of France from Versailles back to Paris, the rise of the salons and of wealthy bourgeois patrons, and the multiplication of social power groups that, because of their variety, were less able than the court had been to mold writers according to a single pattern, were also factors working for the emancipation of the writer. Above all, it was in the eighteenth century that the notion of literary property became more clearly and legally defined and that some writers first succeeded in freeing themselves completely from patronage and in supporting themselves solely by writing for the market. Dr. Johnson in England and Diderot in France are two famous examples of the new breed of independent writer.

The relation between writer and public thus gradually ceased to be the mutual recognition that Sartre considers characteristic of classicism. In some fields of literary production, it is true, notably in tragedy, the earlier relation continued in a weakened form for some time. Voltaire, for example, had his famous triumvirate of Paris friends, all intimately associated with the theater, who commented on his plays and occasionally rewrote passages in order to adapt them to what they considered the taste of the public. The innovations in Voltaire's dramatic writing are in fact extremely prudent and the traditional theatrical conventions of classicism are generally respected if only externally. In the arts, the so-called *connoisseurs* (Mariette, Bachaumont, Caylus) attempted to play a role similar to that of Voltaire's triumvirate. The function of these self-appointed arbiters of taste was basically to mediate between the artist and the public and to maintain in each the common standards and conventions of the neoclassical tradition, thus preventing any departure from what might be called the establishment view of reality, art, truth, and beauty.[25]

By the mid-century, however, these connoisseurs were being left behind, equally disliked by artists who resented their interference and by an expanding public that refused to be represented by them. Their eclipse revealed the eighteenth-century public as more varied, more heterogeneous, less immediately recognizable than that of the previous century. Nevertheless, it was not, in most cases, a mere alien *other,* nor was it so fragmented that the writer could not envisage it concretely and interact with it. Fontenelle, Marivaux, Diderot, and Marmontel were all men of the salons; Fontenelle was also, as secretary of the *Académie des Sciences,* in touch with learned men and scientists throughout Europe. Diderot had a vast circle of acquaintances from all walks of life, notably craftsmen, scientists, and doctors. Voltaire maintained a voluminous correspondence with all kinds of people and he knew that his most trifling *billet* would be read aloud in the salons, copied by countless friends and admirers, and passed eagerly from hand to hand throughout France and Europe. And at Ferney he received the respects of many of those admirers, great and obscure alike, who traveled long distances to see the *patriarche* in person. The eighteenth-century writer thus wrote for a varied public and he probably expected to be read and understood at different levels; yet he still conceived of himself not as a stranger in a foreign land, fated to inevitable misunderstanding, but as a kind of mediator and guide, capable of uniting in himself various aspects of his society and of enriching the humanity of his readers by presenting to them points of view that were not their own. Even Diderot, who as editor of the *Encyclopédie* was aware of and subject to the pressures of the market, did not feel himself alienated from the public. He was, indeed, in his editorial capacity a salaried worker, and although this position freed him both from arrogant patrons and pressing financial worries, it doubtless also chained him to the job as any worker is chained to his job. Nevertheless, it was a job that he wanted to do, that interested him, and that had a real social meaning for him. It often seemed burdensome, but it was never a mere chore, a simple matter of pen pushing, producing for an anonymous and senseless market.

The outstanding example of the alienated writer in the eighteenth century is, as we have seen, Rousseau. Perhaps special circumstances prepared Rousseau for his prophetic role—his virtual orphancy and his situation as a *déclassé* from earliest childhood, his religious apostasies, his exile from his native Geneva, and his life of wandering and persecution. He saw what those who were more rooted in their society could not see or could not accept. Thus his exposure of the history of civilization as a history of violence and repression is a more radical *Kulturkritik* than most writers of the French Enlightenment could produce. While the philosophes unmasked as ideology the beliefs and religions of past humanity, believing that they themselves represented universal reason, he, from his alienation, unmasked this universal reason as itself the ideology of a class.

## LITERATURE AND SOCIETY

We began by inquiring into the relation between literature and its historical context. Perhaps enough has been said to reaffirm the specificity of literary creation as an original mode of human activity, and at the same time to suggest that, along with all other human activities, it is part of social life and thus sensitive, in complex and still rather mysterious ways, to the relations among men in society. Despite its pursuit of "realism" the best eighteenth-century literature, like any other, is more than a mere testimony, however profound and subtle, to a social and historical situation. In those very texts where he most eagerly argues the case for realism, Diderot also scrutinizes the concept of realism and tries to work out an aesthetics that takes account of and encourages the active, shaping role of literature and art. His greatest works, indeed, are not reflections of the given but projections outward into the unknown, and their form is not traditional but original and experimental. Likewise Rousseau's work is not merely a mirror of social life and social problems but something that is added to the social situation and that changes it. Rousseau's entire literary activity was an unrelenting protest against the opposition of subject and object, self and other, fiction or imagination and reality, all of which he saw as distortions created by a repressive civilization. His earliest writing, after the conversion of 1749, was an effort to reach and convert others. Literature was not then a separate realm from reality but an instrument for the transformation of reality, as it had been for many Christian writers before him. Even the later writing in which, despairing of direct action, he turned toward the creation of imaginary worlds and artificial paradises, is no mere reflection of psychological and social disorder. These imaginary worlds expanded in their own way the scope of consciousness and the range of feelings of the eighteenth-century reader. Rousseau's literary experiment, in the novel, in autobiography, in the *journal intime,* did not so much reflect as create a new sensibility in the same moment that they created the forms of expression of that sensibility. As we ponder the relation of literature to society, we should not neglect the active role literature plays in social intercourse and the power its own formal developments have to modify and shape human experience.

## NOTES

1. A recent study of content analysis describes an attempt, in the rather different conditions of modern mass communications, to test the reflection theory (popular attitudes determine communication content) against the control theory (communication content determines popular attitudes) by comparing the proportion of gainfully employed women in magazine stories with that in the actual population from 1900 to 1930. The results, as one might have expected, were inconclusive. "The whole relationship between the content and audience characteristics allegedly 'reflected' in it is far from clear" is the final judgment [Bernard Berelson, *Content Analysis in Communications Research* (New York: The Free Press, 1952)]. See also Diana Spearman, *The Novel and Society* (New York: Barnes & Noble, Inc., 1966). Historians of preliterate peoples have been very concerned with the evaluation of oral testimonies and have warned of the importance of literary stereotypes; see Jan Vensina, *Oral Tradition and Historical Methodology* (Chicago: Aldine Publishing Company, 1965), pp. 15–16, 57–75.
2. "The History of the Echo of Literary Works," in Paul L. Garvin, ed., *A Prague School Reader on Esthetics, Literary Structure, and Style*, Washington, D. C.: Georgetown University Press, 1964, pp. 71–81.
3. Lucien Goldmann, *Recherches dialectiques* (Paris: Editions Gallimard, 1959), pp. 50–51.
4. The argument of the "antihumanist" Marxists appears to be that by positing a *subject* of history—no longer an individual consciousness, admittedly, but a class consciousness—that stands over against it, and is distinct from objective social structures, the "humanist" Marxists remain caught in an idealist metaphysics. For a harsh criticism of Goldmann from this point of view, see Miriam Glucksmann, in the London *New Left Review*, 56 (1969), 49–62.
5. The Russian formalist critics and the Anglo-Saxon New Critics both insisted on the importance of language in literature. For an account of the views of the former, see Victor Erlich, *Russian Formalism* (The Hague: Mouton publishers, 1965), 2nd. ed.; there are extracts from their work in L. Lemon and M. Reis, *Russian Formalist Criticism* (Lincoln, Nebr.: University of Nebraska Press, 1965) and in Tzvetan Todorov, *Théorie de la littérature: textes des formalistes russes* (Paris: Editions du Seuil, 1965). Of the many works by the New Critics, *The Philosophy of Rhetoric* by I. A. Richards (New York: Oxford University Press, Inc., 1936) offers a good introduction. The famous *Theory of Literature*

of R. Wellek and A. Warren (New York: Harcourt Brace Jovanovich, Inc., 1942) synthesizes the two approaches to some extent.

6. In a recent discussion of different methods in the history of philosophy, which seems pertinent to the problems of literary history, Maurice Mandelbaum argues that sociological monism—the view that any element in a society is related to other elements within that society in such a way that it can only be understood through understanding them, and through understanding the society as a whole— makes it impossible in the end to distinguish adequately different cultural series (literature, painting, music, theology, and so on); see *History and Theory*, Supplement 5, 33–66. See also the conflicting positions of Barthes and Goldmann in *Littérature et société: problèmes de méthodologie en sociologie de la littérature* (Brussels: Editions de l'Institut de Sociologie de l'Université Libre de Bruxelles, 1967), notably pp. 34, 35, 38, and 39.

7. "Thematics," in Lemon and Reis, *Russian Formalist Criticism*, pp. 59–95.

8. "Standard Language and Poetic Language" and "The Esthetics of Language" in Garvin, *A Prague School Reader*, pp. 17–69.

9. "Littérature et signification," *Tel Quel*, 16 (1964), 3–17.

10. *Lektsii po struktural'noi poetike* (1964) (Providence, R. I.: Brown University Press, Slavic Reprints, 1968).

11. Cf. Engels's remark at the beginning of *Socialism: Utopian and Scientific*: "We know today that the kingdom of reason was nothing more than the idealized kingdom of the bourgeoisie."

12. On popular culture, see M. M. Bakhtin, *Rabelais and his World*, trans. from Russian by Helene Iswolsky (Cambridge, Mass.: The M. I. T. Press, 1968). On the popular theatre in eighteenth-century France, see Maurice Albert, *Les Théâtres de la foire (1660–1789)* (Paris: Librairie Hachette S. A., 1900).

13. "Molière et la farce," *Revue de Paris*, May, 1901. See also Romain Rolland, *Le Théâtre du peuple* (Paris, 1903), pp. 9–13.

14. On the convulsionaries, see Albert Mousset, *L'Etrange Histoire des convulsionnaires de Saint-Médard* (Paris: Les Editions de Minuit, 1954); on mesmerism, see Robert Darnton, *Mesmerism and the End of the Enlightenment in France* (Cambridge, Mass.: Harvard University Press, 1968).

15. In the Christian, and especially in the Christian bourgeois tradition, Eros frequently appears in the ambivalent form of the attractive and hearty prostitute, such as Dame Douce in *Le Jeu de la feuillée* of Adam de la Halle. A modern example might be Lola Lola in von Sternberg's film of Heinrich Mann's *The Blue Angel*.

16. See especially Diderot's *Éloge de Richardson*. Defending Richardson against the charge that his details are "communs . . . ce qu'on voit tous les jours," Diderot retorts: "Vous vous trompez; c'est ce qui se passe tous les jours sous vos yeux, et que vous ne voyez jamais." (*Oeuvres esthétiques*, ed. Vernière [Paris: Editions Garnier Frères, 1959], p. 35). Of course, the element of "reality" that the writer reminds us of need not be part of everyday social life; indeed, in Diderot's own case this was not so. Diderot also tried to recover the imaginary, the visionary, even the unconscious for "reality."

17. This is also the principal theme of Diderot's writings on the theater, which only a superficial reading, it seems to me, would allow one to categorize summarily as an apology for the "bourgeois" theater. I should even be tempted to argue that Diderot wrote his own "bourgeois" plays largely to provide himself with a good talking point for his general theoretical discussion of a "realistic" theater. His own view of the theater implied, in fact, that good plays could not be written in

the kind of social circumstances in which he himself lived. These circumstances, it seemed, were more appropriate to theoretical discussion and criticism than to creation. A comparison of Diderot with Artaud might be interesting in this respect, though in most ways Diderot is closer in spirit to Brecht. At any rate, Diderot's dramatic work reveals that in the eighteenth century literature could not simply be taken for granted. It had become a problem to itself and was already beginning to take itself as its theme.

18. Roland Barthes, "Image, raison, déraison" in *L'Univers de l'Encyclopédie* (Paris: Les Libraires associés, 1964).

19. The image of the transparent veil that recurs throughout Rousseau's work is surely intimately related to this conception of literature as a utopia in which contradictions are resolved. As a fervent reader of Montaigne, Rousseau had doubtless noted the use of the image in the chapter of the *Essais* entitled "Des vers de Virgile" (Vol. 3, Part 5) to suggest the transforming power by which art "saves" reality from time and reveals it as essence.

20. Mandrou, *De la culture populaire aux XVIIᵉ et XVIIIᵉ siècles* (Paris: Editions Stock, 1964); see also Robert Escarpit, *Sociologie de la littérature* (Paris: Presses Universitaires de France, 1958).

21. David Pottinger, *The French Book Trade in the Ancien Regime 1500–1791* (Cambridge, Mass.: Harvard University Press, 1958).

22. Mornet does, however, risk an estimate of the first edition—4,000 copies; see D. Mornet, "Le Texte de la Nouvelle Héloïse et les éditions du XVIIIᵉ siècle," *Annales Jean-Jacques Rousseau*, 5 (1909), 1–117. See also Mornet's edition of *La Nouvelle Héloïse* (Paris: Librairie Hachette S. A., 1925).

23. See Geneviève Bollème *et al.*, *Livre et société dans la France du XVIIIᵉ siècle* (The Hague: Mouton Publishers, 1965), and the studies of Escarpit and Pottinger.

24. R. Estivals, *Le Dépôt légal sous l'ancien régime de 1537 à 1791* (Paris: Marcel Rivière et Cie., 1961); see also the same author's *Statistique bibliographique de la France sous la monarchie au XVIIIᵉ siècle* (Paris: Imprimerie Nationale, 1965), and several of the studies in *Livre et société dans la France du XVIIIᵉ siècle.*

25. On the connoisseurs, see Albert Dresdner, *Die Entstehung der Kunstkritik* (Munich: F. Bruckmann Verlag, 1915).

# SUGGESTED
# READING
# LIST

## CHAPTERS 1 AND 2:
## SOCIAL, POLITICAL, AND
## ECONOMIC HISTORY

ARIÈS, PHILIPPE, *L'Enfant et la vie familiale sous l'ancien régime*. Paris: Librairie Plon, 1960.

BARBER, ELINOR, *The Bourgeoisie in Eighteenth-Century France*. Princeton, N. J.: Princeton University Press, 1955.

BEHRENS, C. B. A., *The Ancien Régime*. London: Thames and Hudson, 1967.

COBBAN, ARTHUR, *A History of Modern France*, 1: *Old Regime and Revolution*, Harmondsworth, Middlesex: Penguin Books Ltd., 1957.

DAKIN, DOUGLAS, *Turgot and the Ancien Régime in France*. London: Methuen & Co., Ltd., 1939.

FORD, FRANKLIN, *Robe and Sword: the regrouping of the French aristocracy after Louis XIV*. Cambridge, Mass.: Harvard University Press, 1953.

LABROUSSE, C. E., *La Crise de l'économie française à la fin de l'ancien régime et au début de la Révolution*. Paris: Presses Universitaires de France, 1943.

LACROIX, PAUL, *XVIIIe siècle: institutions, usages et costumes*. Paris: Firmin-Didot Etude, 1875.

LE BRAS, G., *Etudes de sociologie religieuse*. 1. Paris: Presses Universitaires de France, 1955.

LEFEBVRE, GEORGES, *The Coming of the French Revolution*, trans. R. R. Palmer. Princeton, N. J.: Princeton University Press, 1949.

LEVASSEUR, E., *Histoire des classes ouvrières et de l'industrie en France avant 1789*, 2nd ed., 2 vols. Paris: A. Rousseau, 1901.

MANDROU, ROBERT, *La France aux XVIIᵉ et XVIIIᵉ siècles*. Paris: Presses Universitaires de France, 1967.

MARION, MARCEL, *Dictionnaire des institutions de la France aux XVIIᵉ et XVIIIᵉ siècles*. Paris: Editions A. & J. Picard & Cie., 1923.

————, *Histoire financière de la France depuis 1715*, 1: *1715–1789*. Paris: A. Rousseau, 1927.

MOUSNIER, ROLAND, and C. E. LABROUSSE, *Le XVIIIᵉ siècle: Histoire générale des civilisations*, 5. Paris: Presses Universitaires de France, 1953.

PERNOUD, RÉGINE, *Histoire de la bourgeoisie en France*, 2. Paris: Editions du Seuil, 1962.

PITSCH, MARGUERITE, *La Vie Populaire a Paris au XVIIIᵉ siècle d'après les textes contemporains et les estampes*. Paris: Editions A. & J. Picard & Cie., 1949.

PRÉCLIN, E., *Le Jansénisme du XVIIIᵉ siècle et la Constitution Civile du Clergé*. Paris: J. Gamber, 1928.

ROTHKRUG, LIONEL, *Opposition to Louis XIV: the political and social origins of the French Enlightenment*. Princeton, N. J.: Princeton University Press, 1965.

SAGNAC, PHILIPPE, *La Formation de la société française moderne*, 2. Paris: Presses Universitaires de France, 1946.

SÉE, HENRI, *La France économique et sociale au XVIIIᵉ siècle*. Paris: Librairie Armand Colin, 1925. Trans. *Economic and Social Conditions in France in the Eighteenth Century*. New York: Alfred A. Knopf, Inc., 1927.

SNYDERS, GEORGES, *La Pédagogie en France aux XVIIᵉ et XVIIIᵉ siècles*. Paris: Presses Universitaires de France, 1965.

SOBOUL, ALBERT, *La France à la veille de la Révolution*, new ed. Paris: Société d'Edition d'Enseignement Supérieur, 1966.

DE TOCQUEVILLE, ALEXIS, *The Old Regime and the French Revolution*. Garden City, N. Y.: Doubleday & Company, Inc., 1955.

*La Vie populaire en France du moyen âge à nos jours*, 4 vols. (devoted to work, leisure, the home, and man). Paris: Editions Diderot, 1964.

## CHAPTER 3:
## ENLIGHTENMENT

BECKER, CARL, *The Heavenly City of the Eighteenth-Century Philosophers*. New Haven, Conn.: Yale University Press, 1932.

BELIN, J. P., *Le Commerce des livres prohibés à Paris de 1750 à 1789*. Paris: Librairie Classique Eugène Belin, 1913.

CASSIRER, ERNST, *The Philosophy of the Enlightenment*, trans. F. C. A. Koelln and J. C. Pettegrove. (German original, Tübingen: J. C. B. Mohr [Paul Siebeck] 1932.) Princeton: Princeton University Press, 1951.

DESNÉ, ROLAND, *Les Matérialistes français de 1750 à 1800*. Paris: Editions Buchet Chastel, 1965.

DIECKMANN, HERBERT, *Le Philosophe: texts and interpretation*. St. Louis, Mo.: Washington University studies—new series: Language and Literature, 18, 1948.

EHRARD, JEAN, *L'Idée de nature en France dans la première moitié du dix-huitième siècle*. Paris: Service d'Edition et de Vente des Productions de l'Education Nationale, 1963.

FOUCAULT, MICHEL, *Histoire de la folie à l'âge classique*. Paris: Librairie Plon, 1961.

———, *Les Mots et les choses*. Paris: Editions Gallimard, 1966.

GAY, PETER, *The Enlightenment: an interpretation*, 2 vols. New York: Alfred A. Knopf, Inc., 1969.

GROETHUYSEN, B., *The Bourgeois: Catholicism versus Capitalism in Eighteenth-Century France*, trans. Mary Ilford. (German original, Tübingen: Max Niemeyer Verlag, 1927–1930.) New York: Holt, Rinehart and Winston, 1968.

HAMPSON, NORMAN, *The Enlightenment* (Pelican History of European Thought, 4). Harmondsworth, Middlesex: Penguin Books Ltd., 1968.

HAZARD, PAUL, *The European Mind, 1680–1715*, trans. J. L. May. (French original, Paris: Boivin et Cie, 1935.) New York: World Publishing Company, 1964.

———, *European Thought in the Eighteenth Century*, trans. J. Lewis May. (French original, Paris: Boivin et Cie, 1946.) New York: World Publishing Company, 1963.

HORKHEIMER, MAX and T. W. ADORNO, *Dialektik der Aufklärung*. New York: Social Studies Association, Inc., 1944. Amsterdam: Em. Querido's Uitgeverij N. V., 1947.

MACPHERSON, C. B., *The Political Theory of Possessive Individualism: Hobbes to Locke*. Oxford: Clarendon Press, 1962.

MAUZI, ROBERT, *L'Idée de bonheur dans la littérature et la pensée françaises au XVIIIe siècle*. Paris: Librairie Armand Colin, 1960.

MORNET, DANIEL, *Les Origines intellectuelles de la Révolution française, 1715–1787*, Paris: Librairie Armand Colin, 1933.

PALMER, R. R., *Catholics and Unbelievers in Eighteenth-Century France*. Princeton, N. J.: Princeton University Press, 1939.

PROUST, JACQUES, *Diderot et l'Encyclopédie*. Paris: Librairie Armand Colin, 1962.

ROGER, JACQUES, *Les Sciences de la vie dans la pensée française du XVIIIᵉ siècle*. Paris: Librairie Armand Colin, 1963.

STAROBINSKI, JEAN, *The Invention of Liberty*, trans. B. C. Swift. (French original, Geneva: Editions d'Art Albert Skira, 1962.) Geneva: Editions d'Art Albert Skira, 1964.

VERNIÈRE, P., *Spinoza et la pensée française avant la Révolution*, 2 vols. Paris: Presses Universitaires de France, 1954.

WADE, IRA O., *The Clandestine Organization and Diffusion of Philosophic Ideas in France from 1700 to 1750*. Princeton, N. J.: Princeton University Press, 1938.

## CHAPTER 4:
## LITERATURE AND SOCIETY

AUERBACH, ERICH, *Mimesis: the representation of reality in Western literature*, trans. W. Trask. (German original, Bern: A. Francke, 1946.) Princeton, N. J.: Princeton University Press, 1953.

BARTHES, ROLAND, *Writing Degree Zero*, trans. A. Lavers and C. Smith. (French original, Paris: Editions du Seuil, 1953.) London: Jonathan Cape Ltd., 1967.

BOLLÈME, GENEVIÈVE *et al.*, *Livre et société dans la France du XVIIIᵉ siècle*. The Hague: Mouton et Cie, 1967.

BRUNOT, FERDINAND, *Histoire de la langue française*, Vol. 6, 1930; Vol. 6, part 2 (by Alexis François), 1932–33; Vol. 7, 1926; Vol. 8, 2 parts, 1934–35. Paris: Librairie Armand Colin.

BURKE, KENNETH, *The Philosophy of Literary Form*. Baton Rouge, La.: Louisiana State University Press, 1941. Reissued New York: Random House, Inc., Vintage Books, 1957.

DARNTON, ROBERT, "Reading, writing, and publishing in eighteenth-century France: a case study in the sociology of literature," *Daedalus*, Winter, 1971, pp. 214–57.

DUMAZEDIER, JOFFRE and JEAN HASSENFORDER, "Eléments pour une sociologie de la production, de la diffusion et de l'utilisation du livre," *Bibliographie de la France*, June 15, June 29, and July 6, 1962.

ESCARPIT, R., *Sociologie de la littérature*. Paris: Presses Universitaires de France, 1958.

———— *et al.*, *Le Littéraire et le social: éléments pour une sociologie de la littérature*. Paris: Flammarion et Cie, 1970.

GARVIN, PAUL L., ed., *A Prague School Reader on Esthetics, Literary Structure, and Style*. Washington, D. C.: Georgetown University Press, 1964.

GOLDMANN, LUCIEN, ed., *Littérature et société: problèmes de méthode en sociologie de la littérature*. Brussels: Editions de l'Institut de Sociologie de l'Université Libre de Bruxelles, 1967.

HATIN, EUGÈNE, *Histoire politique et littéraire de la presse en France*, 3 vols. Paris: Poulet-Malassis et de Broise, 1859 (vol. 2, 149–479 and vol. 3 on "la presse littéraire aux XVIIe et XVIIIe siècles").

*Histoire générale de la presse française*, Publiée sous la direction de Claude Bellanger, Jacques Godechot, Pierre Guiral, et Fernand Terrou, 2 vols., (vol. 1 on eighteenth century). Paris: Presses Universitaires de France, 1969.

LEMON, L. and M. REIS, eds. *Russian Formalist Criticism*. Lincoln, Nebr.: University of Nebraska Press, 1965.

MANDROU, ROBERT, *De la Culture populaire aux XVIIe et XVIIIe siècles: la Bibliothèque Bleue de Troyes*. Paris: Editions Stock, 1964.

NISARD, CHARLES, *Histoire des livres populaires*, 2 vols. Paris: E. Dentu, 1864.

POTTINGER, DAVID, *The French Book Trade in the Ancien Régime, 1500–1791*. Cambridge, Mass.: Harvard University Press, 1958.

SARTRE, JEAN-PAUL, *What is Literature?*, trans. B. Frechtman. (French original, Paris: Editions Gallimard, 1947.) New York: Harper & Row, Publishers, 1949.

WELLEK, RENÉ and AUSTIN WARREN, *Theory of Literature*. New York: Harcourt Brace Jovanovich, Inc., 1942.

# INDEX

145